Byrne's
Complete
Book of
Pool Shots

Byrne's Complete Book of Pool Shots

350 MOVES EVERY PLAYER SHOULD KNOW

Robert Byrne

A Harvest Original • Harcourt, Inc.

ORLANDO   AUSTIN   NEW YORK   SAN DIEGO   TORONTO   LONDON

Requests for permission to make copies
of any part of the work should be mailed
to the following address:
Permissions Department, Harcourt, Inc.,
6277 Sea Harbor Drive, Orlando, Florida
32887-6777.

www.HarcourtBooks.com

Library of Congress
Cataloging-in-Publication Data
Byrne, Robert, 1930–
Byrne's complete book of pool shots:
350 moves every player should know/
Robert Byrne.
p.   cm.
Includes bibliographical references.
ISBN 0-15-602721-6
1. Pool (Game)
I. Title: Complete book of pool shots.
II. Title.
GV893.B97 2003
794.7'3—dc21
2003005599

Text set in ITC Stone Serif Medium OS
Designed by Kaelin Chappell

Printed in the United States of America
First Edition
K J I H G F E

To Pat Fleming
For his many contributions
to the game

CONTENTS

8 BACKSPIN

9 STUN

10 RAIL FIRST

11 BANKS

ACKNOWLEDGMENTS

For assistance in rounding up the graphics presented in this book, I wish to thank Heinrich Weingartner, editor, billiard table manufacturer, room owner, and curator of the Weingartner Billiard Museum in Vienna, Austria; Dieter Haase of Kessel, Germany, author of *Das Billardspiel, Eine Bibliographie* (*Billiard Games, A Bibliography*), which gives the details in German on more than 2,000 books on carom and pocket billiards; Brad Morris of New Deco, Boca Raton, Florida, purveyor of billiard memorabilia; Mike Shamos, author of *The New Illustrated Encyclopedia of Billiards,* college professor, attorney-at-law, and curator of The Billiard Archive in Pittsburgh, Pennsylvania; photographers George Bennett and John Grissim; artist Cynthia Nelms-Byrne (my wife); my editor at Harcourt in San Diego, California, Jen Charat; and my agent for twenty-five years in New York, Knox Burger.

—Robert Byrne

INTRODUCTION

Dan Louie breaks the balls at
the 1998 Sands Regency
Tournament in Reno, Nevada.
Photo by George Bennet,
George Bennet Photography

Except for the opening review of fundamentals, this is not a book aimed primarily at beginners. Terms like "scratch," "stroke," and "object ball," are not defined. Little space is given to teaching the student how to stand at the table, which end of the cue to chalk, or how to form a bridge. You won't find a chapter on the rules of games.

While instruction is offered throughout the book on follow, draw, English, massé, jumps, and other techniques, the emphasis is on special shots, shots that are not widely known and, in some cases, very nearly unknown. Even if you already have a library of pool books and magazines and consider yourself well informed, you'll find shots here that you've never seen before. A few, in fact, were invented during the course of compiling this book. By the time you turn the last page, your arsenal for winning games will be greatly expanded. Some of the shots are surprisingly easy to make. Knowledge is often the key rather than exceptional skill.

Not all the shots are unfamiliar. Many of the sections begin with relatively easy shots and progress to more difficult and unusual examples. To create a book useful to players of all skill levels, I have included a sprinkling of shots discussed in my videotapes and earlier books on the game. The easier shots provide a base for the advanced material and make it unnecessary for the reader to refer to other works. However, for those who want more information on certain types of shots, references are provided in the text.

No book on pool can be complete, for the game is infinite. There are some 350 shots described herein, and each one has endless variations. But it's not the exact ball placements in the diagrams you should be concerned with in most cases, it's the idea behind the shot. Understand the idea and you'll be able to apply it in a wide variety of positions.

I've included a few shots that aren't practical in important games. Some depend on unnatural positions you'll never see in real life or are simply too hard to make with any consistency. They're included because they are interesting, even amazing, and because they demonstrate the range of possibilities on a pool table. What is practical, after all, depends on the circumstances. A shot too tough to try in a money game or in a tournament might be just the ticket in a pastime game. Make a fantastic one-in-million shot and you'll remember it for the rest of your life. You'll never make one if you never try, and the time to try is when you are playing for fun.

Some of the low-percentage shots are good for challenges ("Give me five tries and I'll bet I can make this shot . . .") or for exhibitions of trick shots. With practice, the percentage won't be so low.

This book will provide you with new ways of winning as well as new ways to enjoy one of the world's greatest and most enduring games.

Robert Byrne
Dubuque, Iowa
(e-mail: bob@byrne.org)

Byrne's Complete Book of Pool Shots

BASICS 1

A toy store trading card from 1886. The game being played is a form of
bagatelle and the caption reads: "Mayest thou thy Christmas happily begin/And
ne'er despair shouldst thou not always win."

While this book is aimed mainly at players who can already handle a cue fairly well, there is always the possibility that it will fall into the hands of a beginner. For that reason, I will start with a brief review of fundamentals. Newcomers to the game should take a lesson or two from a qualified instructor and read one or more of the many fine instructional books now available, some of which I wrote myself. Getting past the beginner stage is impossible unless you know how to stand, hold the cue, stroke, and aim, and there's more to those seemingly simple acts than you might think.

If you are unfamiliar with pool instructional materials and have never studied the game before, a good place to start is with *Byrne's New Standard Book of Pool and Billiards,* which covers fundamentals in much more detail than you will find here and which continues to advanced concepts. If you'd rather watch than read, try *Byrne's Standard Video of Pool, Volume I* and *Volume II.* Both are available at billiard supply stores. Short descriptions of these and other books and tapes can be found on my Web site at *byrne.org.*

Getting Started Right

An important tip   The most important tip is the one at the end of your cue. If it flattens out or mushrooms, trim it with a razor blade and sand it off so it is flush with the sides of the ferrule (the plastic collar onto which the tip is glued). Be very careful not to scratch or sand the ferrule or the wood of the shaft.

Hold it   Hold the cue as level as possible unless you are deliberately trying to make the cueball curve or jump. When the tip is halfway from the cueball to your bridge hand during your warm-up strokes, your right forearm (assuming you are right-handed) should be aimed straight down at the floor. Hold the cue firmly but not tightly.

Chalk up Applying chalk to the tip before every shot is not too often, but it's not necessary to chalk up so frequently when hitting the cueball in the center. If the tip won't hold chalk, rough it up with a piece of sandpaper or one of the many scuffers designed for the job. Don't spin the cue into the chalk; instead, rock the chalk back and forth on the tip or brush the flat surface of the chalk across the tip.

Crouch Some top players bend down so low when aiming that their chins touch the cue. Most have their chins no more than a foot above the cue. If you are having trouble pocketing balls, it may be that you aren't bending over far enough to aim the cue like a rifle.

Aim Really aim, don't just go through the motions. One way is to imagine where the cueball must be at the moment of contact with the object ball, then aim through the center of the imagined cueball. Another way is to keep refining your aim until the hit looks right, neither too thick nor too thin. Fans of geometry and precision might like the method explained in Diagram 1.

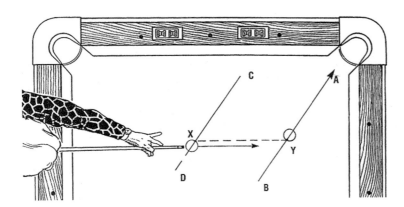

1 The geometry of aiming

If you have trouble aiming cut shots, resorting to geometry might help. Find point *Y* on the object ball directly opposite the target, *A*. Imagine The line *BYA*. Imagine line *DXC*, parallel to the first line, passing through the center of the cueball. *X* is the point where the line intersects the left edge of the cueball. To make the shot, point *X* on the cueball must hit point *Y* on the object ball. Aim the cueball along a line parallel to line *XY*.

On every shot that's not straight in, an allowance for throw must be made. "Throw" is the term used to describe how a shot is thrown slightly off line by the frictional forces during the collision. For more, see Section 5.

Follow straight through   The tip is only in contact with the cueball for one milli-second. What you do with your cue after that can't affect the cueball, but you should develop the habit of following straight through. If your cue normally rises after contact or swerves toward the side of the English, then you will have a harder time hitting the cueball exactly where you want to and will miscue more often than you should. To develop a straight stroke, try picking a spot on the cloth six inches or so beyond the end of the cue and making the cue tip stop directly on it or above it after hitting the cueball.

Stay down   During your warm-up strokes and when hitting the cueball, don't bob your head or move anything except your forearm. Let the cue follow straight through, then freeze until the cueball is well on its way. Extraneous body movement during the stroke makes precision pool impossible. Your elbow should remain frozen in space until the end of the follow-through.

Watch your eyes   When aiming, your eyes will move back and forth a few times between the cueball and the object ball. Almost all top players have their eyes on the object ball—or a point of aim on a cushion—when they pull the trigger. An exception might be on a very easy shot where the critical factor is the amount of spin on the cueball; then you might focus on the cueball to make sure you hit it where you want to.

Beware of English   A majority of shots can be made without any spin (English) on the cueball. Four problems arise when hitting the cueball off-center left or right. One is "squirt," which causes the cueball to travel slightly off line in a di-rection opposite the English. Another is that a cueball with sidespin will throw the object ball off line because of the friction between the balls during contact. The third is that unless the cue is exactly level, the cueball's path will curve on its way to the target. Finally, using more than a little sidespin increases the chances of a miscue. On the other hand, English is essential on some shots in order to get a good shot at the next ball.

Sidespin has little effect on the angle the cueball takes off the object ball, but it can greatly change the angle of rebound off a rail. What affects the angle the cueball takes off the object ball are backspin (draw) and topspin (follow).

Follow and Draw

Follow and draw are essential elements in cueball control. Both depend on hitting the cueball above or below center on the vertical axis, although sidespin can be applied as well. You'll learn the technique faster if you understand a bit of the underlying physics.

Follow   If a cueball rolling naturally down the table strikes an object ball full in the face, the cueball will stop dead in its tracks for an instant, then its continuing rotation, which is reduced but not eliminated by the impact, will cause the cueball to move forward, "following" the object ball.

When the cue tip strikes the cueball halfway from the center to the top (to be precise, 70 percent of the diameter up from the bottom) on the vertical axis, the cueball will start with natural roll immediately. Natural roll means that there is no slippage between the ball and the cloth. While it is possible to hit the cueball *slightly* higher than 70 percent of its diameter without miscuing, it is impossible to demonstrate in practice that doing so will create extra topspin. In other words, for practical purposes it is impossible to strike a cueball so high that it begins its movement with more rotation than natural roll. The distance the cueball rolls after it hits an object ball, then, (provided the 70 percent point is where the tip hit the cueball) depends only on how hard the cueball is struck.

Scientist and pool buff George Onoda noticed an interesting fact about striped pool balls: ordinarily the width of the stripe is exactly half the diameter. (Do note, however, that some balls on the market today have wider stripes.) This permits an easy method of learning how to apply maximum spin. Use a striped ball as a cueball. Orient the stripe so that it is exactly horizontal. The upper edge of the stripe is exactly halfway from the center of the ball to the top. Clean the ball, chalk your cue, and practice hitting the top edge of the stripe. After each try, examine the ball and see if the chalk mark left by the tip is on the edge of the stripe.

There are several training cueballs on the market now that make it easy to practice maximum spin shots. The one made by Elephant Balls has a red dot surrounded by a red circle with a diameter equal to half the width of the ball. Position the red dot so that it is on the equator of the ball (halfway from the cloth to the top of the ball); the red circle marks the maximum spin striking point for follow, draw, and English. Keep in mind that hitting the cueball that far off center increases the danger of miscuing (see Diagram 81).

Forward curves   What happens when you use maximum follow on a cut shot? The cueball caroms off the ball along a path at right angles to the object ball's path, then bends forward in a parabolic curve. The sharpness of the curve depends on the fullness of the hit and the speed of the ball. You can see examples of these paths diagrammed in *Byrne's New Standard Book of Pool and Billiards* (1998), page 55, or traced in slow motion on *Byrne's Standard Video of Pool, Volume II.*

Much of the artistry of the game depends on the ability to judge the cueball's curving path on follow and draw shots, both for maximum and less-than-maximum off-center hits. For examples, see Sections 7 and 8.

Draw   If you have absorbed the foregoing, it will come as no surprise that maximum draw, or backspin, results from a hit that is halfway from the center of the cueball to its resting point on the cloth. Trying to hit lower than that greatly increases the chance of a miscue. If the bottom edge of the cue tip hits the cloth first, for example, a miscue is almost a certainty. The best way to find out what a maximum low hit looks and feels like is to use a striped ball as the cueball with the stripe horizontal. During your warm-up strokes, try to direct the upper edge of the tip toward the low edge of the stripe, and after hitting the cueball, retrieve it and see where the chalk smudge is.

To further reduce your chances of miscuing on maximum draw shots make sure that your tip is properly shaped and groomed and is well chalked; your bridge should be snug and hold your cue close to level. Players who have trouble getting lively draw action almost always aren't hitting the cueball low enough (see Section 8, Diagram 101). Another frequent flaw that prevents lively draw action is not hitting the cueball hard enough when the cueball is more than a couple of feet away. Beginners should practice short straight-in shots with the cueball only six or eight inches from the object ball. At that distance, it is easy to learn how to make the cueball draw back several feet without hitting it hard.

Stop   On straight-in shots, a cueball that slides into the object ball with neither topspin nor backspin will stop dead. It takes practice and a certain touch to shoot stop shots at all distances. On long, straight shots, considerable backspin must be applied, otherwise the friction of the cloth will reduce the backspin to zero and allow the cueball to begin rolling before it reaches the object ball. Some players consider the stop shot the most important shot in pool.

Sidespin

Sidespin, or English, has little effect on the angle the cueball takes off the ball it hits. That angle is influenced by topspin and backspin. What sidespin mainly does is change the way the cueball bounces off a rail. Being able to judge the altered rebound angle accurately is essential for position play.

Because of squirt, throw, and swerve, it is much harder to pocket a ball when English is used than with a centerball hit. Top players, however, have an uncanny ability to accommodate and exploit these three variables.

Players differ in their estimates of how often cueball spin must be used, but it is probably less than 20 percent of the time. For the great majority of shots in pool, the cueball can be controlled adequately by using centerball hits and varying the speed or "cheating the pocket" (driving the object ball into one part of the pocket or another).

Rebounds   One way to learn how to judge the effect of sidespin on cushion rebound angles is to practice with a cueball only. For example, shoot the cueball down the centerline of the table and by using various amounts of sidespin try to make it bank into any desired point on the side rails, which can be marked with coins or balls. Drills like this get boring fast, so it's best to do them as competitive games with a friend.

English throw   It's not quite accurate to say that the cueball should hit the object ball at a point directly opposite the pocket. That's correct advice if throw is ignored. "Throw" is the term used to describe the way the cueball can push an object ball off line because of the friction between the balls at the moment of impact. Right English throws the object ball slightly to the left, and you must allow for it. The reason is that the leading edge of the cueball is moving to the left, and when that moving surface hits the object ball, it grabs and throws it off line to the left. The same explanation applies to the way a frozen two-ball combination is thrown off line if the first ball is hit on the side.

Cut-shot throw   Throw occurs on cut shots, but it is difficult to see. If you are cutting an object ball to the left, left-hand sidespin will require a slightly thinner hit than you would need if no sidespin were used. Right-hand spin will throw the object ball to the left, so a slightly thicker hit is required. Throw occurs on cut shots even if no English is used because the surface of the cueball rubs against the object ball, creating a frictional force. No throw occurs if the spin on the cueball is such that it rolls off the object ball instead of rubbing against it. For a full discussion of cut-shot throw complete with diagrams, see *Byrne's Advanced Technique* (1990), pages 23–27. The throw effect in general is covered in detail in *Byrne's New Standard Book of Pool and Billiards* (1998), pages 83–102.

To see how much harder it is to make a shot when sidespin is used, set up a long diagonal straight-in shot with the object ball in the center of the table and the cueball four feet away. Try to make it with heavy left or right English. If you can make a long, straight shot half the time with no English, you'll be lucky to make it one time in five with English.

Squirt   Another factor that makes English dangerous is deflection, now usually called "squirt." As mentioned already, when you hit a cueball right or left of center, it won't travel in a direction exactly parallel to the cue; it will diverge slightly in a direction opposite of the English. Cues that have small diameter tips (between 11 and 12 millimeters) cause less squirt than fatter ones (between 12 and 13 millimeters) because there is less weight near the end of the shaft to push the cueball off line. Most good players unconsciously adjust for the squirt when using English and many aren't aware that there is such a phenomenon. One cuemaker, Predator, reduces squirt by drilling a small hole down the axis of the shaft at the tip end to reduce the weight. Front end weight can also be reduced by making the ferrule shorter (Schuler) or thinner (Meucci).

Swerve   A third factor that makes it harder to pocket balls when English is used is swerve. Unless the cue is exactly level, English will make the cueball's path bend slightly. The more you elevate the back of the cue, the more the cueball will curve, or swerve. Because the cue is elevated at least slightly on the great majority of shots, swerve must be considered when English is applied. There are, of course, situations when swerve (technically massé) is needed to bend the cueball around an interfering ball.

Conclusion   Use just enough sidespin to get the job done. A quarter inch off center is usually plenty.

Safety Play

Even though defense is as important as offense, especially in nine-ball, you almost never see anybody practicing defense. Laying down a good safety often requires an accurate hit and careful control of speed, as well as good judgment on carom and rebound angles. You can't acquire those skills without practice.

Ball in hand anywhere on the table is a devastating penalty for a foul in nine-ball, especially when combined with the loss-of-game rule for three fouls in a row. Ball in hand anywhere is also becoming more common in eight-ball—for example, see the "World Standardized Rules" as set out in the Billiard Congress of America's rule book. Playing safe is often the best move to make even when the table is relatively open. (Warning! Make sure you know the local eight-ball rules, which vary widely.)

Here's a condensed checklist of points to remember:

1. Coming to the table with the freedom to place the cueball anywhere, you naturally think offense. Think defense also, because the same freedom can enable you to completely bury the cueball.

2. With ball in hand and a cluster that must be broken, consider playing safe in a way that breaks up the cluster. It may be possible to drive a ball into the cluster and at the same time snooker your opponent. Such a double-duty safety immediately turns the game in your favor. See the examples of "aggressive defense" in Section 20.

3. Practice what snooker players call the "stun run-through." Hit the object ball full in the face while striking the cueball just slightly above center. The result is that the object ball travels a long way and the cueball creeps forward only a few inches . . . very useful in safety play. For examples, see Section 9.

4. In nine-ball, if you are snookered and have very little chance of hitting the lowest-numbered ball, consider taking a foul by bumping one ball against another to create a cluster and make it harder for your opponent to run out.

5. In nine-ball, when the 9 is in the jaws of the pocket, strategy changes completely. Search for ways to make the 9 with a combo or a carom. Don't forget the option of pocketing the 9 directly if you have no decent shot. Better to make your opponent run out than to give him an easy combo or carom.

6. In eight-ball don't try to run out unless you are pretty sure you can, because if you are left with one or two balls while your opponent has five or six, you are at a great disadvantage. The table is cluttered with balls that are interference to you and opportunities for your opponent. Instead of making a ball, it might be better to block a pocket with it, reducing options for your opponent and leaving you an easy position shot later.

7. In eight-ball, let's say one of your opponent's balls is jawed, thus making a runout for you almost impossible. Consider making his ball by softly driving one of yours into it, thus replacing his ball with yours. Your inning is over, but, depending on the position of the other balls, you may have greatly improved your position. Even caroming the cueball off one of your balls into his jawed ball can be a strong play. The cueball is left in the jaws, which may be a terrible leave for your opponent.

8. In eight-ball, it is sometimes worth making one of your opponent's balls directly, even though your opponent gets ball in hand. Make the move when he or she has only one or two balls left and they are tied up. If you still have a lot of balls on the table, there may be no way for your opponent to run out, play safe, or avoid a sellout.

9. Under most rules of eight-ball, you can pocket one of your balls and end your inning by announcing "safety" before you shoot. It's rare that you would want to do that, but there are situations when it is the best play. Let's say you have only one ball you can make, but no way to get position on the next ball. It's easy to think of layouts where calling safe and making a ball will leave your opponent nothing.

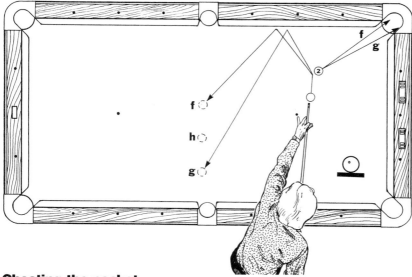

2 Cheating the pocket

Shoot this shot three times with exactly the same English and speed and the cueball will land on three different spots, depending on the hit. A full hit that sends the 2-ball to the left side of the pocket will stop at *f* in the center of the table. If the 2-ball enters the middle of the pocket, the cueball will roll a little farther and stop at *h*. The thinnest possible hit on the 2-ball that still puts it in the pocket sends the cueball to *g*. The three hits carom the cueball off the 2-ball along three different lines; because of interfering balls, only one might be usable in playing position.

A player who tries to send the ball to *f* in the center of the table and ends up at *g* instead might say, "I shot too hard." It's just as accurate to say, "I hit the 2 too thin."

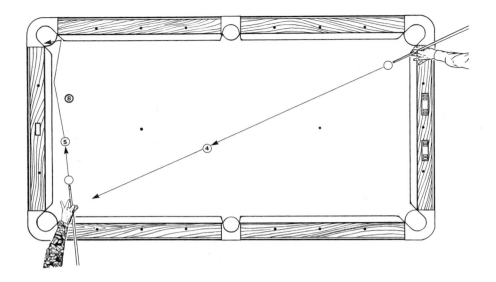

3 Accuracy versus slop

A long, straight shot with the object ball halfway from the cueball to the pocket presents the smallest possible margin of error and is therefore a good one to practice. Your mechanics have to be very good to make such a shot consistently.

At the left, the 8-ball is in the way of the 5-ball. Shoot firmly and the ball will rattle in the jaws and not go in. The best chance to make it is to shoot so softly that the 5-ball just barely reaches the pocket. Unless the pocket is very tight, the ball will drop after bouncing lightly off one or both faces of the jaws.

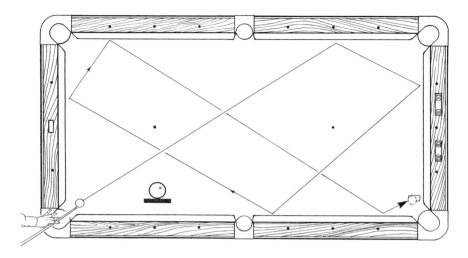

4 Speed control—I

One place where speed control is the only thing that counts is the lag for break, but it is important on almost every shot. An interesting game that will improve your touch is to place a sheet of typing paper anywhere on the table and try to land the cueball on it after a bank of three or more rails. Shoot until you fail, always starting from wherever the cueball stops. The same sequence of rails can't be used twice in a row. When you fail, your opponent shoots. Whoever reaches ten successes first wins. As a solo test, keep track of how many shots it takes you to land on the paper ten times.

In the diagram, the idea is to bank the cueball off six rails and make it come to rest on a dollar bill. With half an hour of secret practice, you'll be able to impress your friends.

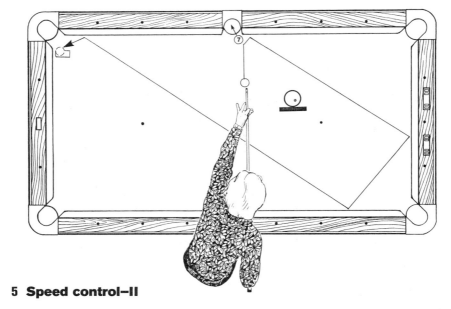

5 Speed control–II

In nine-ball, you frequently will have to make a ball and send the cueball off several rails for position. Here's a shot you should try a few times. Cut the 7-ball in and, depending on your level of skill, put the cueball on a sheet of typing paper, a half a sheet, a quarter of a sheet, or a dollar bill.

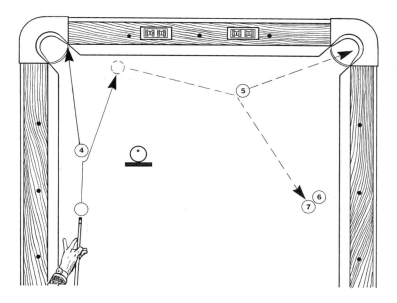

6 Getting an angle

One of the keys to running balls is getting an angle. Not only must you make the first ball, you must get an angle on the next ball that permits you to get to the third one. In other words, you must plan three shots ahead. If there is a cluster that must be broken, the task becomes getting an angle on a ball that can be used as a break ball. In the diagram, the 6-7 must be separated. To do it, follow forward softly on the 4-ball, leaving the cueball in a position to carom into the cluster while cutting the 5-ball into the corner. A good nine-ball player would spot the possibility at a glance even with five other balls on the table and might make the 1-, 2-, and 3-balls in a way that leaves the diagrammed position.

FOULS 2

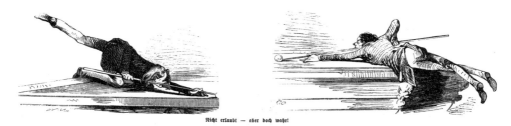

Nicht erlaubt — aber doch wahr!

No fair! Kneeling, crawling, lying down, or sleeping on the table is a foul.

Courtesy Heinrich Weingartner, Weingartner Museum of Billiards

Foul strokes are the main causes of arguments in pool games. Did the tip of the cue hit the cueball twice? Did the cueball hit the object ball twice? When the gaps are small and the speed is fast, it's sometimes impossible to tell for sure whether the stroke is legal or not. You've got to feel sorry for the referee of a crucial tournament match who must make a ruling on an unclear shot.

Many fouls can be controlled by the shooter, so, knowingly or not, someone can gain an advantage or win the game by violating the law. The readers of this book, of course, would never cheat. The following examples of what is fair and what is foul are offered to help you guard against players whose knowledge and morality are inferior to your own.

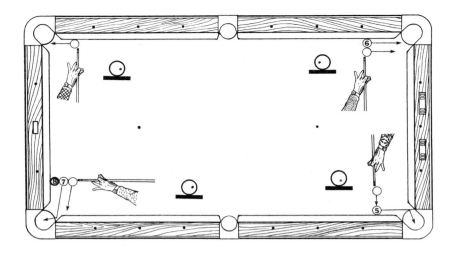

7 Push-shot fouls

You can't simply place the tip of your cue against the cueball and push, although some interesting effects are possible when you do. The bare-bones idea is seen at the upper left, where the cueball is frozen to the cushion a half diamond from the corner pocket. Press the tip against the right side of the cueball, push forward, and it will squirt left into the pocket. At the upper right, left sidespin sends the 6-ball to the right. Use two object balls, as shown at the lower left, and the one in the middle can be forced into the pocket by using right English. All three shots are fouls because contact between the tip and the cueball is "maintained for more than the momentary time commensurate with a stroked shot," to quote the stilted language of paragraph 3.24 of *The Official Rules and Records Book*, published by the Billiard Congress of America.

The shot at the lower right is legal. The 5-ball can be forced into the corner with low right English provided the 5 isn't too far from the corner. This shot is fairly easy on a bar table where the cueball is generally heavier than the object ball. On some cushions, the shot occasionally works when the frozen ball is several feet from the corner.

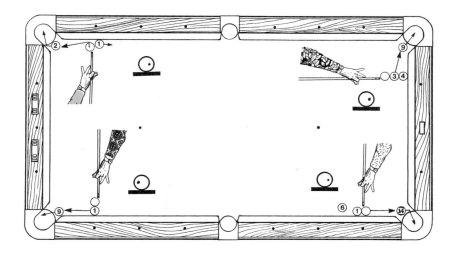

8 More push-shot fouls

At the lower right is an application of the first shot in the previous diagram. The game is eight-ball, and the player wants to pocket the 14-ball without having to shoot left-handed over the top of the 1-ball. Pushing the cueball into the 14-ball with right spin is clever but illegal. At the upper right and lower left are shots that would win games of nine-ball if push shots were allowed.

The sneaky foul at the upper left is Wimpy's Pinch, credited by Willie Jopling to the late, great hustler and tournament player Luther "Wimpy" Lassiter. It's a double-hit foul. Push the cue straight forward with a soft stroke—the cueball rebounds from the rail, is struck again by the advancing cue tip, and is redirected toward the 2-ball. The double hit is too fast for the eye to see.

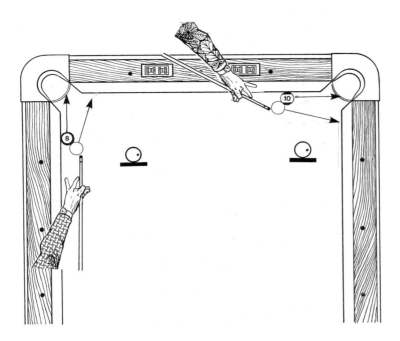

9 Still more push-shot fouls

Here are two push shots of a different type. It looks impossible that the 8-ball or the 10-ball can be made in the corner pockets, and they can't if you use a normal stroke. In each case, place the tip of the cue against the cueball as shown, use outside English (English on the side away from the object ball) and push straight through. The tip stays in contact with the cueball long enough to herd the object ball into the pocket.

Shots like these are obviously fouls, but a particularly scurrilous opponent, or one who doesn't know any better, might try one against you in a game. If someone begins aiming in a way that will almost certainly result in a foul, stop the action and explain why such a shot is illegal. Eternal vigilance is the price of victory.

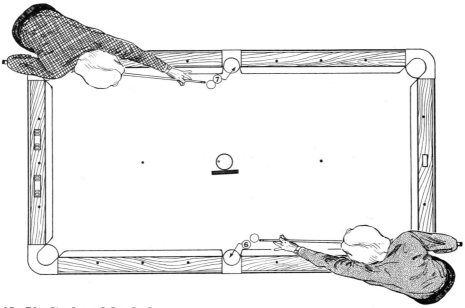

10 Shafted and fouled

At the top, the 7-ball is frozen both to the rail and the cueball. With a normal stroke, but with the tip of the cue hitting the 7-ball so far left of center that a miscue is guaranteed, you can make the 7 in the side by following straight through and using the side of the cue shaft to shove the ball into the pocket. At slow speed, the foul is obvious, but at high speed it's hard to tell what happened. Don't let it be done to you.

The shot at the bottom is more difficult, as well as more deceptive. The cueball is not quite touching the 6-ball. With extreme left English, it is possible to make the tip of the cue hit the cueball first and then the 6-ball, knocking it sideways into the pocket. Do it right and there is no telltale click of wood against ball, which in the previous shot announces that a heinous crime has been committed.

Let me say again that these fouls are explained for your protection, not so that you can start a life of crime yourself.

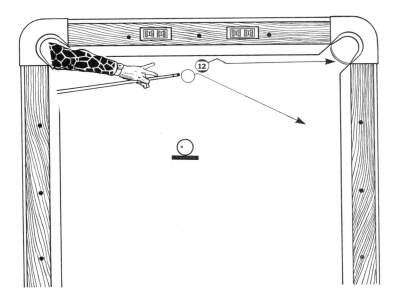

11 A double-hit foul

There's a well-known foul shot in which a long follow-through enables the player to hit the cueball, knock a blocking ball to one side, and hit a second ball with the cue tip, pocketing it. The shot, which is quite easy, can be seen at the right side of Diagram 24. Diagrammed above is a difficult variation in which the first ball bounces off the rail to be struck again by the tip of the cue. Use speed and the second hit happens too quickly to be seen. Note that the follow-through has to be at least six inches long.

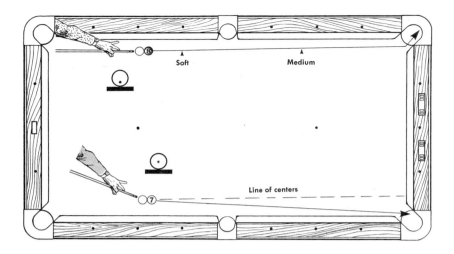

12 Fair push shots

When the cueball is frozen to an object ball, it's within the rules to shoot into it, provided you make a normal stroke and don't start with the tip touching the cueball. At the bottom, note that the line of centers doesn't run into the pocket. The 7-ball can be made easily. Aim toward the rail as shown. The friction at the contact point between the two balls will throw the ball off line and into the pocket. (Throw is explained at length in *Byrne's New Standard Book of Pool and Billiards* [1998], pages 83–101.)

If the line of centers formed by the two frozen balls runs directly into the pocket, as at the top, you can make the 8-ball without allowing the cueball to follow it in by hitting the cueball below center. The arrowhead shows roughly where the cueball will stop with soft backspin. A medium stroke with backspin will send the cueball farther down the table. The way the cueball can be made to chase the object ball toward the pocket and stop dead in its tracks is surprising to beginners. If you have trouble getting the stop action with a level cue, raise the butt and shoot slightly downward. Make sure your tip is well chalked.

For more on throw, see the examples in Section 5.

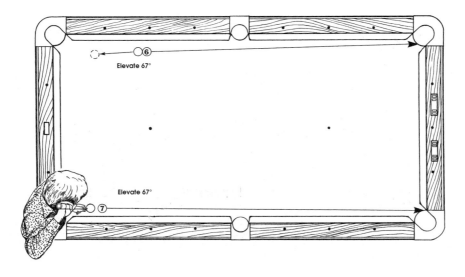

Elevate 67°

Elevate 67°

13 Two massé shots

The cueball–6-ball combination at the top is straight in. You can make the 6 and draw the cueball back by raising your cue to somewhere around 67 degrees from horizontal. There is nothing magical about 67 degrees—it simply means that you should elevate about halfway between 45 degrees and 90 degrees. (To be technical, the label in the diagram should read 67½ degrees, but that level of precision is obsessive-compulsive.) At that angle, the cueball will advance several inches before coming back. Elevate much higher and the 6-ball may not be given enough speed to reach the pocket. A difficulty with this shot is avoiding sidespin on the cueball; precise placement is very hard to judge with a cue raised so high. Sidespin will throw the object ball off line to one side or the other.

At the bottom there is a small gap between the balls. It's not easy with a level cue to hit the 7-ball hard enough without hitting the cueball twice. Shooting down at the cueball from a steep angle reduces the chance of the double-hit foul, but you must remember to lift your cue out of the way quickly or the cueball will come back and touch the tip again.

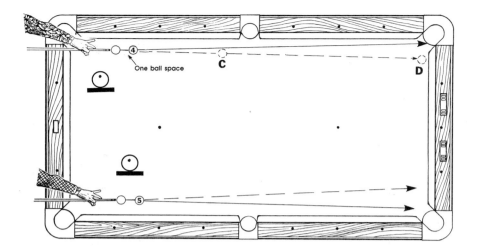

14 How to spot a double hit

When a cueball hits an object ball full in the face, it stops. If it has topspin or backspin, it will follow or draw after an instant's hesitation. At the top there is one ball space between the two balls. If you can restrict your follow-through to two inches or less, it's easy to make the 4-ball in the corner and cause the cueball to follow all the way down the table to D. On a fair shot, the cueball will have reached the vicinity of C when the 4-ball disappears into the pocket. That's the proof that there was no double hit: the object ball goes much faster down the table than the cueball.

At the bottom is the same shot. If you follow through three inches or more, you'll hit the cueball again and the two balls will travel down the table at close to the same speed. The closely matched speeds shout, "Foul!" If your opponent shoots a double-hit follow, voice your objection and demonstrate on another table how you know it was a foul.

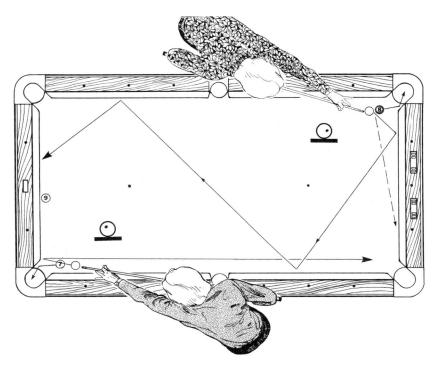

15 Two deceptive double-hit fouls

Watch out for the shot at the lower left. The cueball is one ball width away from the 7-ball. Your treacherous opponent wants to make the 7 and get the cueball to the other end of the table. That's not easy with a legal hit. But hit the 7 head on—with or without topspin—and follow through and the cueball is hit twice and banks the length of the table like magic. What makes the position deceptive is that the object ball is close to the pocket. There is no time to gauge the relative speeds of the two balls because the 7 disappears immediately. The shooter might not even realize that he has fouled. To see the difference between fair and foul, place the cueball eight inches away from the 7 and see how hard it is to get the cueball to the other end of the table using topspin.

At the top right is a related foul. The gap between the balls is only a quarter of an inch. Cutting the 8-ball in with a thin legal hit will send the cueball along the dashed tangent (right-angle) line. Shooting into the 8-ball with outside English, as the player is doing in the diagram, guarantees a double hit. The cueball will push through the 8-ball illegally and zigzag down the table as pretty as you please for perfect position on the 9-ball.

TECHNICAL NOTE: In geometry, a tangent is a line that touches a circle; it necessarily forms a right angle with a radius that intersects the contact point. In pool, when a rolling ball collides with a still ball, the balls diverge along paths that form an angle close to 90 degrees, a useful concept when playing position. The terms "tangent line" and "right-angle line" are used here interchangeably.

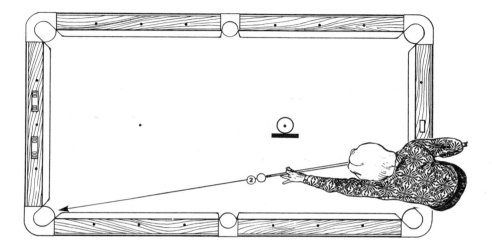

16 The grip-hand stop

Here the 2-ball is straight in, but the gap between the cueball and the object ball is so small that it is practically impossible to make the 2 without hitting the cueball twice. There is an old trick for avoiding the foul. Carefully position the cue tip a hair from the object ball and align the cue along the correct aiming line. Without moving the cue, slide your grip hand forward until it is snug against the edge of the table. Now when you make a backswing and bring the cue forward, the flesh of your grip hand will hit the table and compress just enough to permit the tip to hit the cueball. Smacking your hand against the side of the table (*ouch!*) reduces the follow-through to near zero.

This technique can be used in a wide range of positions because the grip hand can be placed anywhere from the butt end of the cue to a couple of feet from the tip.

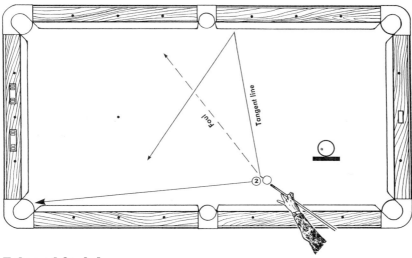

17 Fair and foul—I

Another way to handle a straight-in small-gap shot is to treat it as a cut shot, using throw to keep the object ball on the scoring line. Left-hand English not only reduces the chance of a double-hit foul (right spin is almost a sure foul), it also causes throw that compensates for the cut. Don't hit the cueball above center or it might bend forward into the side pocket.

If the shot is fair, the cueball will travel along the tangent line, which, as you can see, is close to a right angle with the path of the object ball. If the shot is foul, the cueball will travel *ahead* of the tangent line.

Keep in mind that follow or draw on the cueball (topspin or backspin), will make its path curve away from the tangent line, but not in the first few inches after contact. The curves are demonstrated on *Byrne's Video of Pool, Volume II.*

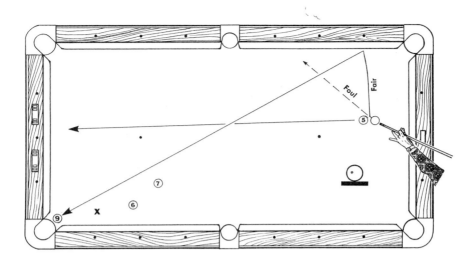

18 Fair and foul—II

The 9-ball is hanging on the lip. In a pastime game, you could try to make it instead of playing safe. Use high left on the cueball. The inside English avoids the foul and high makes the cueball path bend slightly forward. Even if you miss, proper speed will leave the cueball near X, hidden from the 5-ball, which will bank back to the right end of the table.

If it is your opponent who is shooting, watch to make sure the cueball isn't pushed ahead of the tangent line with a double hit.

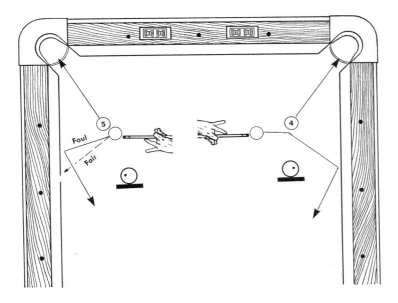

19 The cut-shot foul

At the right is a simple cut shot with the cueball six inches from the object ball. Using outside (right, in this case) English for positional reason presents no problem. At the left is the same cut angle, but with the distance between the balls reduced to a quarter inch. Outside English will result in a foul unless you can stop the cue at the instant of impact. The double hit will force the cueball partly through the space occupied by the 5-ball along the line marked "Foul." In shots of this type, a foul can be avoided by using inside (on the side toward the object ball) English, unless the gap is very small and the line of aim is too much into the object ball (a thick, rather than a thin, hit).

Whether or not a foul occurs on small-gap cuts can be determined by noting the path of the cueball. If the cueball leaves the object ball along a path that is at right angles to the object ball's path, all is fair.

The double hit is often hard to detect, but the shooter can "feel" the foul because of the slight vibration of the two rapid-fire contacts between the tip and the cueball.

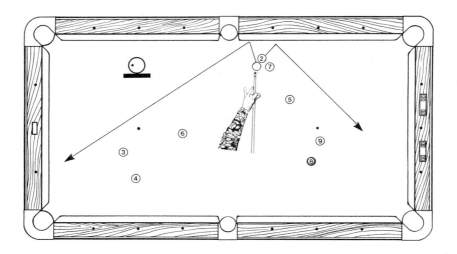

20 Avoiding a scratch—I

A well-informed player with no conscience can make use of the cut-shot foul in several ways. One is to avoid scratching. Here your opponent in a game of nine-ball has decided to play safe by sending the 2-ball to the right and the cueball to the left. A very thin hit not only doesn't move the 2-ball far enough, it is a cinch scratch in the side. Understanding the mechanics of the cut-shot foul, however (perhaps by reading my article about it in the March 2002 edition of *Billiards Digest* magazine), he aims for a half-ball hit, sending the cueball partly through the object ball and avoiding the scratch as shown.

Don't let him get away with it.

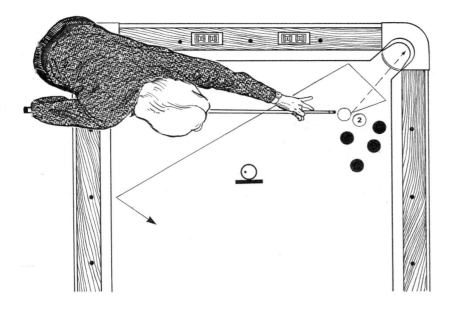

21 Avoiding a scratch—II

Your contemptible adversary in this case has decided to play safe by sending the 2-ball into a cluster of balls and banking the cueball three rails to leave you in a pickle. One little problem is that hitting the 2-ball thin sends the cueball directly into the corner pocket. Because she thinks you don't know any better, she aims for a semi-full hit and relies on the double-hit to miss the scratch and send the cueball around the table as planned.

I hope you are paying attention, because what I'm telling you can save you a lot of money.

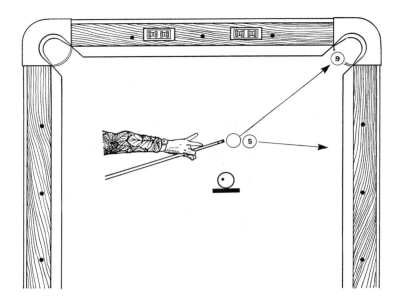

22 Foul to score

If the cueball were a few inches away from the 5-ball, it would be easy to make the 9-ball by caroming the cueball off the 5. With a small gap between the balls, the only legal way to make the carom is with a massé shot, hard to reach so far from a rail. Which brings us to the illegal way. Shoot into the 5-ball as shown. Outside (left) English assures a double hit and a path for the cueball that is far from the tangent line.

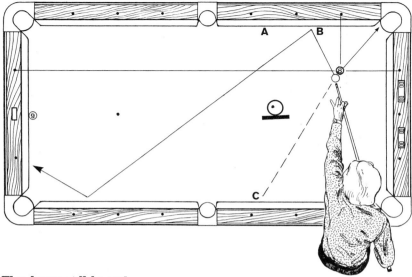

23 The impossible cut

An almost unknown side effect of the cut-shot foul is that a ball can be cut thinner than is possible with a legal hit. To get the feel of this particular felony, examine the diagram. The 8-ball is at the intersection of the first diamonds. The line of centers passes through the third diamond from the corner, marked *C,* and the gap is an eighth of an inch. The goal is to cut the 8-ball in and get position on the 9-ball at the other end of the table. The position just barely allows the shot to be made with an extremely thin hit, but the speed required will send the cueball to the left end of the table and back to the right end. However, cuing the ball as shown with outside English sends the 8-ball into the corner pocket and the cueball to *B* at *slow speed* (instead of along the legal right-angle line to *A* at high speed) and down the table for position on the 9-ball. The foul can be felt by the holder of the cue as a slight vibration and the sound is a bit suspicious, too, but who would know it's a foul and have the nerve to call it?

The shot is demonstrated on my *Gamebreakers* video available from billiards supply dealers or from Accu-Stats Video Productions.

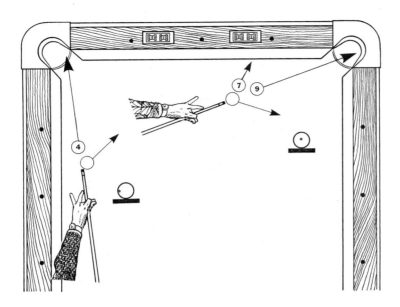

24 Two optical illusion fouls

At the left is a hand-is-quicker-than-the-eye miscue foul I am ashamed to have invented because it might be used to cheat somebody. Aim at the center of the 4-ball as if the cueball weren't there. The position is such that the tip of the cue will just barely graze the side of the cueball, sending it to one side as the cue follows straight through to bang the 4-ball into the pocket. I use the word "bang" to indicate that high speed should be used to make the foul harder to see.

The foul at the right is as old as the hills. Aim through the 7-ball at the 9-ball. Shoot hard to disguise what happens and use a long follow-through. The cueball deflects to the right, the 7-ball is cut to the left, and the cue advances to strike the 9-ball and bang it into the pocket.

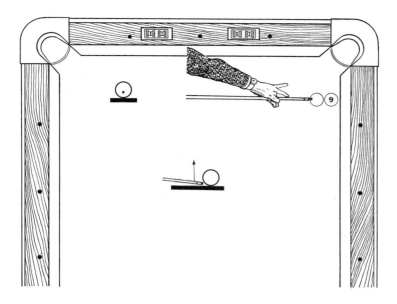

25 The lift-brush foul

On very rare occasions, a problem arises that has no good solution. The 9-ball is not quite frozen to the rail or the cueball. If the 9-ball were frozen to the rail, then to satisfy the rules, it would have to be driven to a different rail to complete a legal safety. Here a player with superhuman skill might be able to delicately send the 9-ball into the rail by shooting straight at it without hitting the cueball twice. During the 1990s, somebody came up with what I call the lift-brush foul. Place the tip of the cue under the cueball. Instead of moving the cue forward as you would to put backspin on the cueball, lift the tip straight up, barely brushing the cueball. The 9-ball is driven to the rail, the cueball has hardly moved, no double hit has occurred, and while you haven't improved your chances of winning, you haven't sold out. Be advised that in most jurisdictions the stroke has been ruled abnormal and hence illegal. Maybe not in your home, though, when you are trying to avoid losing to your little sister.

CAROMS **3**

In this book caroms are defined as shots in which an object ball is driven into a second object ball. In the next section are billiard shots, in which the cue-ball caroms from one object ball to another.

Although many carom shots appear at first glance to be easy, nobody is as comfortable when using a ball rather than a pocket as a target, so aiming takes a bit more concentration.

REMEMBER THIS: A moving ball bounces off a still ball along the tangent line.

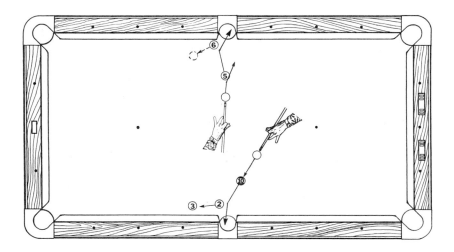

26 Solving and creating problems

At the top of the diagram is an easy and obvious carom shot. Instead of playing the 5-ball straight into the side, carom it off the 6-ball to send the 6 to a more favorable place. This is as simple as it gets.

At the bottom is a position from a game of eight-ball. You have the stripes. Why carom the 10-ball off the 2-ball? To put your opponent's 2-ball in a less favorable place. With luck, you will create a problem cluster with the 2 and 3.

NOTE: As with most of the diagrams in this book, other balls that might be on the table in a real game are omitted to make the underlying principle stand out more clearly.

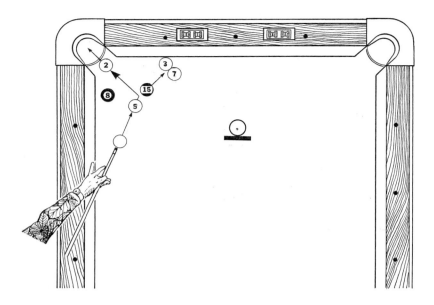

27 Cluster busting

The game is eight-ball. You have the solids. You could easily cut the 5-ball into the 2-ball, but the cueball will run away to parts unknown. A better choice is to carom the 5-ball off the 15-ball to pocket the 2, stopping the cueball. The main virtue of playing the carom is that the 3-7 problem cluster will be broken apart.

The position in this diagram is arbitrary and will never occur exactly as shown, but the principle is something to remember and consider whenever a ball is hanging on the lip.

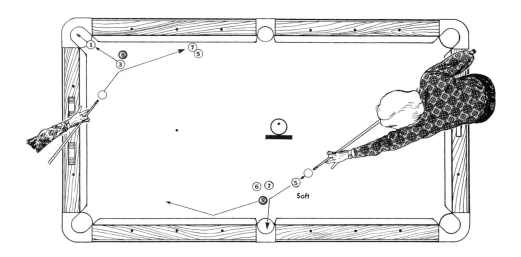

28 More cluster busting

Here are two eight-ball maneuvers. At the top, making the 1-ball directly fails to break up the 7-9 cluster. Caroming the 3-ball off the 8-ball sends the cueball into the cluster.

At the bottom, the shooter can cut the 5-ball cleanly into the side, but position on the 6-ball and 7-ball for the same side pocket is impossible because the 8-ball is in the way. A solution is to carom the 5-ball off the 8-ball. A soft stroke and a high hit will send the cueball forward a foot or so for position on the 6 and 7 in the opposite side pocket. The point to remember is that a carom can sometimes be used to clear away a blocker ball.

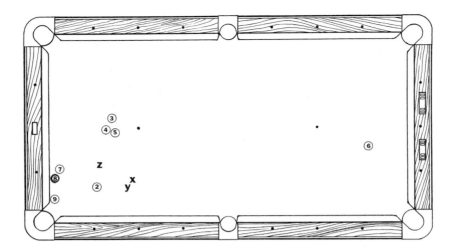

29 A game winner

Your opponent has fouled in a game of nine-ball, giving you ball in hand. Where would you put the cueball? You could put it at point *x* and try to drive the 2-ball into the right edge of the 9-ball, cutting it in. Considerable precision is required. A better solution is to place the cueball at *z* and glance the cueball off the 2-ball into the 9.

Even better yet is to put the cueball at point *y* and drive the 2-ball into the left half of the 8-ball. The 2-ball will carom off the 8 and pocket the 9. There are a lot of safety plays worth considering, especially if your opponent is already on one foul (three fouls in a row loses the game). But the carom shot is almost a cinch in the given position.

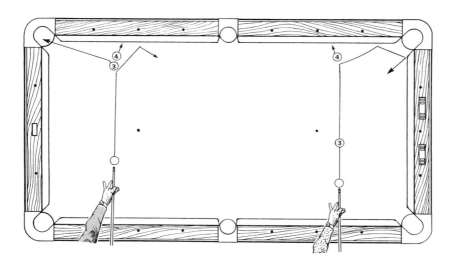

30 The distance factor

In both of the diagrammed shots, the 3-ball caroms off the side of the 4-ball at the same angle and speed. The shot at the left is easy; the shot at the right isn't, and not just because it is harder to be precise at a distance. The problem is that the 3-ball at the right has time to pick up natural roll. After hitting the 4-ball, the topspin will bend the ball path forward as shown. To combat that, you must hit the 3-ball very hard so it won't be rolling freely when it hits the 4-ball. At the left, two balls are so close together that the 3-ball will *slide* into the 4-ball and will stay on the right-angle line without bending.

Another reason that carom shots are easier when the two balls are close together is that the right-angle line is obvious.

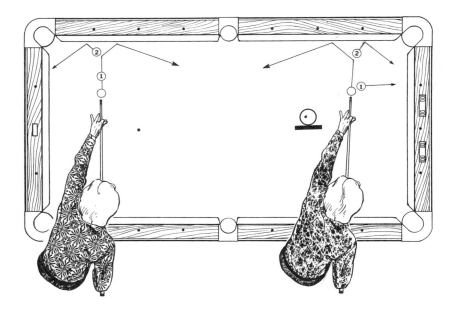

31 Two safety plays

At the left, the player has decided that cutting the 1-ball in the corner or car-oming it into the corner off the left side of the 2-ball doesn't lead to anything useful because of the way other balls (not shown) are arranged. A possible safety play is to send the 1-ball to the other end of the table by caroming it off the right side of the 2-ball. In some positions like this, the cueball can be drawn back a few feet to bury it behind some blockers.

NOTE: If a ball hits another at a half-ball angle (the extended ball path of the moving ball touches the edge of the still ball), they will diverge at right angles and *at the same speed.* Realizing this will help you predict the final resting places of both balls.

At the right is a billiard shot. A thin hit on the 1-ball sends the cueball off the left side of the 2-ball. A little left sidespin and the cueball goes down table for a safety. There are endless positions that could be diagrammed in which a carom or a billiard off a second ball is the best choice. The key is a setup in which the cueball can be controlled and the proper hit on the second ball can be made with accuracy.

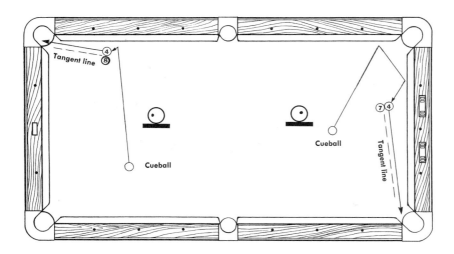

32 Rail-first caroms

When two balls are frozen, the tangent line runs from the contact point at right angles to the line of centers formed by the two balls. At the left, going off the rail into the side of the 4-ball will send the edge of the 4-ball along the tangent line into the pocket as shown. The shot is so easy that you can afford to adjust the speed and the English to get good position on the next ball.

At the right is a similar shot, but one that is best approached two rails first. It's not difficult even if the cueball is at the other end of the table, provided that you are sure the tangent runs into the pocket.

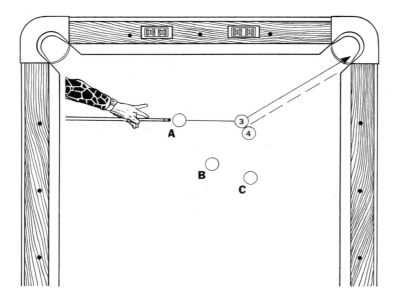

33 The tangent line

My high school geometry teacher would call the dashed line shown in the diagram the perpendicular bisector of the line of centers. You and I call it the tangent line, or the right-angle line. Note that the 3- and 4-balls are positioned so that the tangent line hits the point of the pocket. From position *A,* it's hard to miss the 3-ball unless you hit it somewhere on the left side.

From position *B,* please note, it is difficult, but not impossible, to hit the 4-ball first and make it in the corner because the edge of the ball will travel along the tangent line. The shot can be made only by hitting the far right edge of the 4-ball, getting what I call push-through action.

Put the cueball at *C* and hit the 4-ball full in the face and hard, and it's easy to send it into the pocket because of push-through action. Backspin on the cueball isn't strictly necessary, but speed is. With enough backspin and speed it is possible to send the 4-ball into the end rail instead of the pocket.

If you don't practice shots like these once in a while, you have no reason to complain if you miss one in an important game.

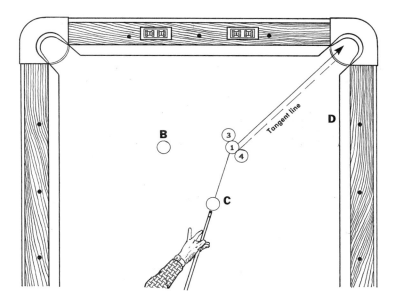

34 The three-ball carom

Set up three balls as shown, put a cueball at *C,* and ask a friend if the 1-ball will go into the pocket if struck softly. She may very well say no because the tangent line from the contact point between the 1- and 3-balls hits the rail at *D,* far from the pocket. The 1-ball, in fact, goes right in. Hit the 1-ball from position *B,* however, and it will follow the wrong tangent line.

What happens in this three-ball mystery shot is that the ball taking most of the cueball's energy gets out of the way and allows the other ball to determine the middle ball's path. The principle is used in many trick shots.

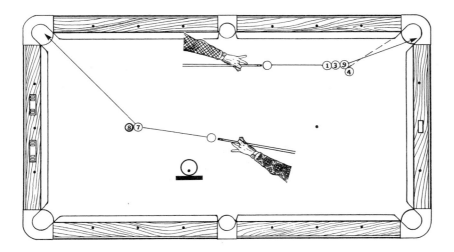

35 Push-throughs

At the right, hitting the 1-ball will send the 9-ball into the pocket off the 4-ball even though the tangent line doesn't seem to be in the right place. Having a ball or two pushing the 9-ball forces it ahead of the tangent line. Try it and see. This shot comes up often in big-cluster games like straight pool.

The ultimate push-through shot is at the left. The 7-ball is on the spot and the 8-ball is behind it and frozen to it. Aim as shown with backspin and high speed and you will occasionally be rewarded. I might try it in a pastime game, but in a tournament, a safety is the wisest course.

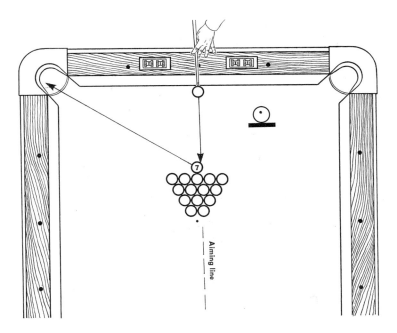

Aiming line

36 The pull-back carom

This is good for challenges and bar bets. Can you make the 7-ball from the given cueball position? Use topspin, shoot medium hard, and hit the 7-ball slightly to one side. Because the 7 is held in place for an instant by the mass of balls, it can be given enough backspin to carom it back into the corner pocket.

Normally, only about 2 percent of the cueball's spin can be transferred to an object ball, but more spin is transferred when the object ball can't escape because the time the two balls are in contact is greater than the customary millisecond.

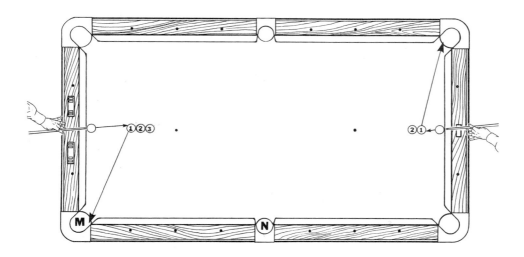

37 Pull-back limits

In my opinion, these two shots are the best that can be done with pull-back action in positions with only one or two balls in supporting roles. They are low-percentage shots and impossible with brand-new or newly polished balls.

At the left, the 1-ball is one diamond from the rail and two balls are frozen to it. On one freakish occasion when I was practicing the shot, the 1-ball backed up into pocket *M* as shown, the cueball banked into side pocket *N,* and the 3-ball somehow banked into pocket *M.* Your balls have to be really dirty for that to happen.

At the right, the space between the cueball and the 1-ball is the width of one ball and there is only a single ball in support. On my table and with my balls, this is the best I could do. With a gap greater than a ball width, the 1-ball can't be made.

A surprising trick shot making use of the pull-back principle can be found in *Byrne's Treasury of Trick Shots in Pool and Billiards* (1982), page 162.

BILLIARDS 4

Ready and waiting.

After a snapshot taken in
Chicago, circa 1975, of Richard
"Baby Brother" Powell, perhaps
the greatest black three-cushion
player in history.

Oil paintings by Cynthia Nelms-Byrne

There is a lot to be said for playing three-cushion billiards once in a while. It will help you become better at judging the exact angle the cueball takes off the object ball; how the cueball path curves on cut shots depending on the angle, the speed, and the spin; how sidespin affects the rebound angle off a rail; and how the cueball travels around the table on multiple-rail shots. In many areas of the country, unfortunately, it's not easy to find a place to play billiards (as distinct from pool).

Three-cushion is played on a five-by-ten-foot table without pockets and with only three balls. To score a point, the player must make the cueball hit both of the other two balls, but before hitting the second ball, the cueball must hit three or more rails. Within that simple definition lies an intriguing world of geometry, imagination, and nuance. For a look at this beautiful and challenging game, see the last section of *Byrne's New Standard Book of Pool and Billiards*. Videotapes of matches between world-class players are available from Accu-Stats Video Productions. (For a free catalog, phone 1-800-828-0397 or go to the Web site: www.accu-stats.com.)

There's a reason why Efren Reyes of the Philippines, arguably the greatest nine-ball player in the world, is so good at escaping from safeties: he's an excellent three-cushion player. Many past champions were superb at both pool and billiards: Alfredo de Oro, Johnny Layton, Ralph Greenleaf, Willie Mosconi, Irving Crane, and Larry "Boston Shorty" Johnson. The best three-cushion player in the world, Torbjörn Blomdahl of Sweden, has played a lot of nine-ball and would be a monster if he turned his mind to it.

In this section we will consider billiard shots that come up in pool.

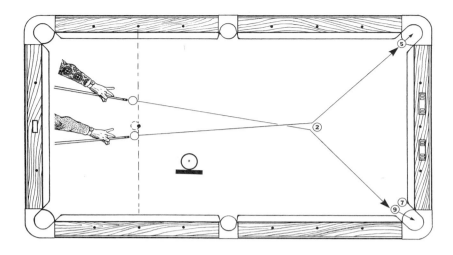

38 The kitchen carom

The carom option as drawn here is quite easy. With the cueball a couple of inches to the right of the spot, a half-ball hit will send it to the center of the 5-ball. Soft speed is in order to avoid following the 5 into the pocket. An advantage is that if you miss, the 2-ball will be nowhere near the hanging ball.

The half-ball carom is especially good when the target balls are not centered in front of the pocket, as is the case with the 7-ball and the 9-ball. To make the 9, place the cueball farther away from the center of the table as shown; to make the 7, place the cueball on the spot.

The beauty of the half-ball hit—in which the extended path of the cueball grazes the edge of the object ball—is that a slight error in aim affects the carom angle hardly at all. (See *Byrne's Advanced Technique in Pool and Billiards* [1990], pages 45–49.)

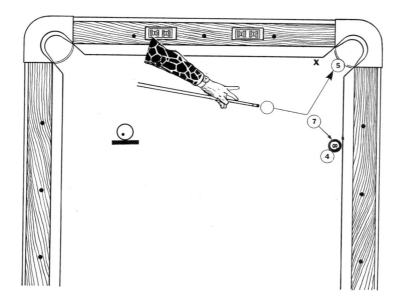

39 Billiard cluster-buster

In a game of eight-ball, you have the solids. The 4-ball and the 8-ball are tied up. One way to score and break up the cluster is to hit the rail at *X,* which will send the cueball off the 5-ball and into the 8-ball. Another move to consider is the one shown, a soft draw of the 7-ball, which will also break up the cluster.

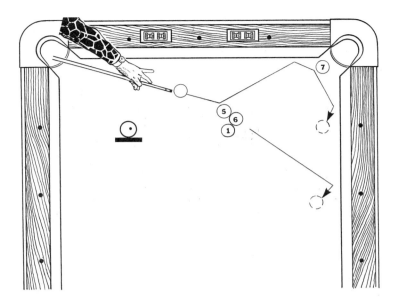

40 Another billiard cluster-buster

You have the solids again. There are two ways to break up the three-ball cluster: either go thin off the right side of the 7-ball and back into the cluster, which isn't bad, or go off the left side of the 5-ball as shown, then to the rail to make the 7, coming to rest near the first diamond. The billiard will almost certainly leave another shot, while going off a rail into a cluster, even a small one, sometimes leaves the cueball stuck against a ball.

When one ball is near the pocket, watch for easy billiard shots like this.

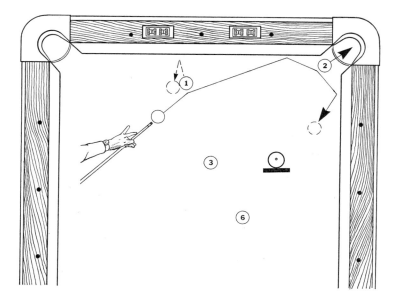

41 Rail first to control the first ball

The game is either nine-ball or rotation, which means you have to hit the lowest ball first, in this case the 1-ball. There are two ways to make the 2-ball. Hitting the 1-ball on the left side and making the 2 on a combination sends the cueball to the other end of the table. In some cases you can make the cueball go up the table and back down for position, but if other balls make that difficult or impossible, consider the billiard shot. I show the 1-ball being hit so thin that the cueball hits the rail before pocketing the 2-ball. A thicker hit on the 1-ball to carom the cueball directly into the 2-ball might bank the 1-ball too far up the table for an easy second shot.

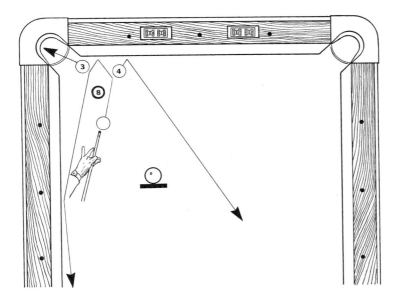

42 Rail first to control the cueball

Let's say you are faced with this position and you want to get the cueball to the other end of the table, or at least leave yourself a shot at the 4-ball after making the 3-ball. A direct billiard requires a full hit on the 4-ball, which creates the possibility of leaving the cueball stuck behind the 8-ball. A thinner hit on the 4 sends the cueball into the end rail before the 3 and then down the table.

The rail-first idea is eminently feasible when the ball is this close to the jaws.

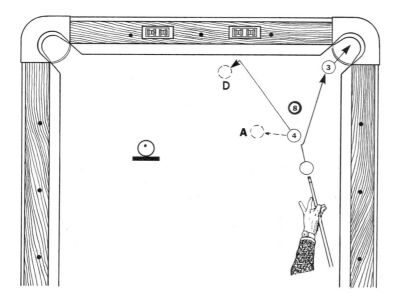

43 The thick or thin choice

When you want to carom off a ball to a certain point, there are often two options. You can either hit the first ball very thin, or hit it full with topspin so that the cueball follows through the ball. Billiard players face that choice routinely; pool players aren't quite so familiar with it.

A simple example illustrates the idea. A thin hit on the 4-ball makes the 3-ball on a billiard but leaves the 4-ball at *A*. A full hit also makes the 3-ball and knocks the 4-ball to *D*, a good place for the next shot.

You could try to hit the 4-ball thin and the 3-ball on the left side so that the cueball will carom to the left for a shot at the 4-ball, but with the follow-through option available there is no need for precision on the billiard.

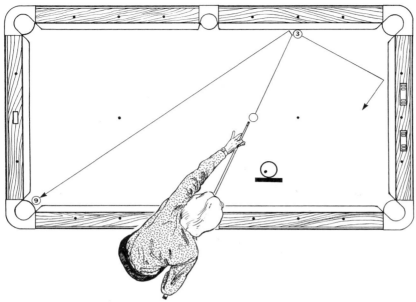

44 **One rail to score**

When the money ball is in the jaws, the game changes completely. Instead of
trying to run the table, you need only to find a combination, a bank, or a billiard to win the game. The one-rail billiard in the diagram is fairly easy, provided
you're a billiard player as well as a pool player. If you never play billiards, then
you must practice shots like this occasionally to get a feel for them. Be sure to hit
the cueball low as well as left at this particular angle. High left will make the cueball's path bend forward and kill the speed. See Diagram 89.

It may be that you will use this pattern to play safe, making use of other
balls that may be on the table. Try it a few times to see the huge difference between high left and low left. For the test, place the balls exactly as shown.

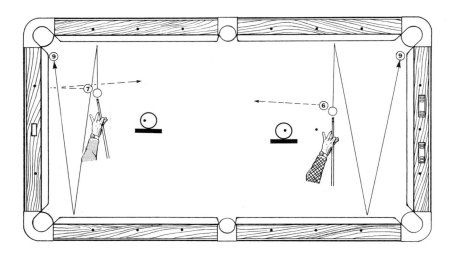

45 Cross-table shots

At the left is a shot three-cushion players call an outside cross-table. In the diagram, the balls are placed so that a direct combination is a possibility, but it would be hard to avoid a foul using a bridge while trying to drive the 7-ball directly into the 9-ball. When shooting the cross-table pattern, make sure you give the 7-ball enough speed to get it out of the way of the returning cueball.

The shot at the left requires considerable English; the shot at the right hardly any. When the cueball goes off the side of the 6-ball, it will pick up a little right English. It's up to you to decide how much more, if any, to apply.

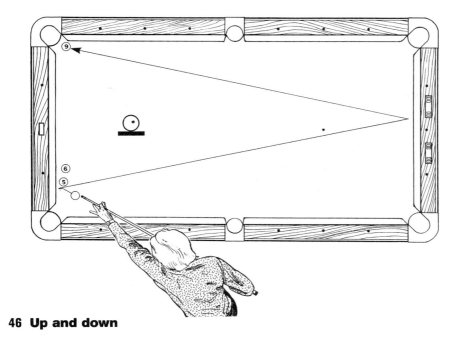

46 Up and down

The game is nine-ball. It's hard to see a good safety in this position. Maybe the best is to hit the 5-ball very thin on the left side and leave the cueball at the right end of the table. But with the 9-ball in front of the upper-left pocket, the up-and-down shot is awfully tempting. You may choose to play safe in the position given, but with more blocker balls on the table, reducing the chances of selling out if you miss, the up-and-down shot is a good choice to consider.

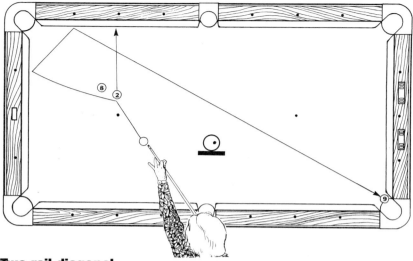

47 Two-rail diagonal

Here is another common pattern in three-cushion. You must blend the hit and the English so that the 2-ball will rebound from the cushion and be out of the way of the cueball as it comes off the second rail. With practice, you can control the cueball's path with considerable accuracy, choosing either to make a jawed ball as shown or to leave the cueball in the lower-right-hand part of the table for a safety.

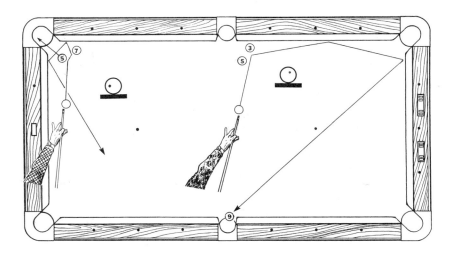

48 Second-ball position

At the left is a common position technique. Use left English, adjust the hit on the 5-ball so that the cueball hits the 7-ball thin on the left side, and the cueball spins out of the corner for position or to break up a cluster.

At the right is a nine-ball position. The 5-ball prevents banking the 3-ball into the 9-ball. One possibility is a safety: you might try hitting the 3 softly on the right side in an attempt to hide it behind the 5. This type of safety is not easy because you have to judge very accurately the travel distance of both the cueball and the object ball. Diagrammed is a shot that ends the game immediately. A top player with billiard experience might make it as often as half the time.

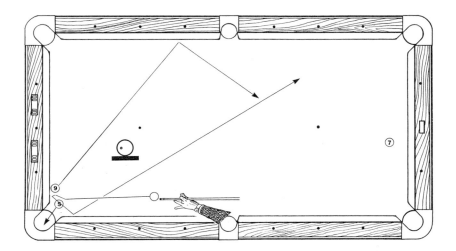

49 **Length of table position**

If you had this layout, would you be able to make the 5-ball and get position on the 7-ball at the other end of the table? It's easy if you can manage to hit the 5 in such a way that the cueball caroms off the edge of the 9-ball. Left English will carry the cueball off two rails to the opposite end. It's another example of using a second ball to get position on a third ball.

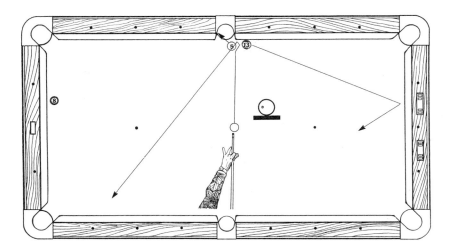

50 Side pocket position

The game is eight-ball. The problem is to make your last ball and get position on the 8-ball at the left end of the table. Fortunately for you, I've drawn the diagram so that the 13-ball is in exactly the right place. There's a big margin of error for making the 5-ball, so you can manage to carom into the left edge of the 13-ball with left-hand spin.

There is a tendency on billiard shots of this type to hit too much of the second ball, thus killing the cueball's speed. Use low left instead of high left. You'll have to try this a few times to get the hang of it.

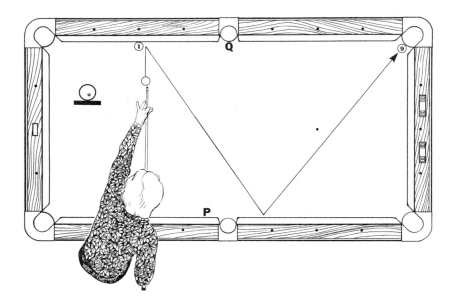

51 Zigzag

It's possible, of course, to hit the left side of the 1-ball with left English and go three rails to make the 9-ball, but that path might be blocked by other balls. A second and more difficult option is the zigzag pattern. As in most billiard shots where you are going off the side of a ball that is frozen to a rail, use low English to avoid high-ball curves.

In the diagram, the 9-ball is made, but you will most often use this pattern to play safe. Don't complain about botching the shot in a game if you've never practiced it.

If the 9-ball is in the jaws of the side pocket at Q, there is no three-cushion shot off the left side of the 1-ball (well, there is with a feather-thin hit and draw-induced curve off the first rail, but that's tough). The best chance to end the game is to hit the 1-ball thin on the right edge and bank the cueball to P and Q.

Patterns like this may strike you as impractical. Whether they are or not depends on how familiar you are with them, whether or not omitted balls will protect you if you miss, and whether or not there is a safety shot that improves your chances of getting a better shot on the 9-ball on your next turn.

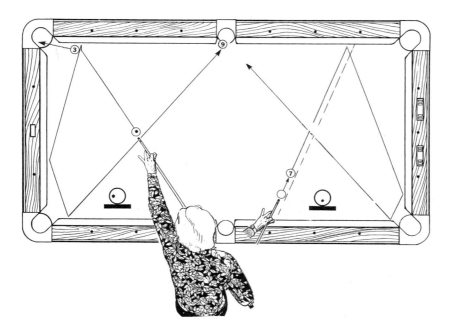

52 Three rails in the side

If you find yourself with the position at the left side of the table (other balls are omitted), you might as well pocket the 3-ball with left-hand English and try for a three-rail bank to the 9-ball at the side pocket. Even if you fail to make the 9, it's still your shot.

At the right side of the table, the dashed line connects the first and third diamonds. That's the limit of a three-cushion side-pocket bank, at least on my table, and it takes a hard stroke to keep the ball from running long. If the object ball is any farther to the left, the shot can't be made. Before trying to bank a ball three rails into the side in a game, check to make sure it is within the limit described by the imaginary dashed line.

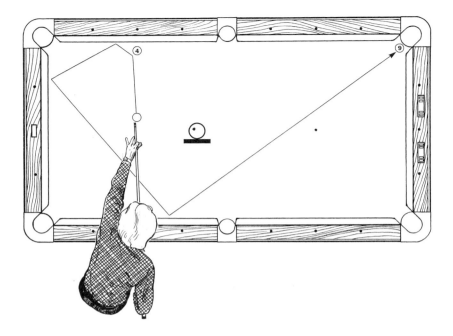

53 Standard three-cushion bank

Here is the basic three-cushion, around-the-table bank shot. Hit about half the 4-ball using high left English with a moderate stroke. Because the 4-ball is not frozen to the rail, there is no need to use low English. The main danger is that the 4-ball will bank across the table and kiss the cueball as it comes off the third rail. You'll never be able to judge the chances of the kiss unless you try the shot a few dozen times. Missing the kiss might require less ball and more sidespin.

This pattern is more often used for safety than for scoring. With practice, you can learn to leave the cueball just about anywhere in the upper-right portion of the table.

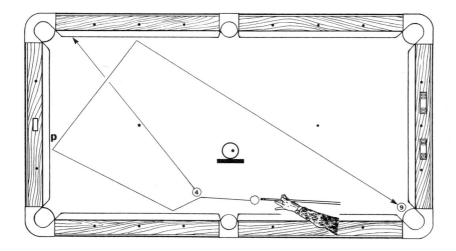

54 Long angle, three cushions

Here is another standard three-cushion shot. Interfering balls often, but not always, rule out around-the-table shots like this. The 4-ball can be hit thick or thin provided the cueball hits near point *p* on the second rail. You have to be able to judge whether or not there will be a kiss where the ball paths intersect; such judgment comes only with practice.

As usual, this pattern can be used for defense as well as offense.

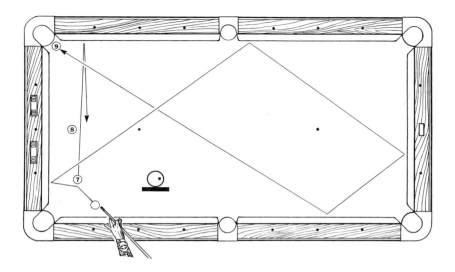

55 Four rails

In a game of nine-ball, how would you handle this position? There are a number of safeties that can be tried, but nothing is easy. The four-rail around-the-table shot is for those who want to go out in sensational fashion, but it's difficult. You have to hit the 7-ball thin so the cueball loses hardly any speed, and you have to come close to the upper side pocket without scratching. The shot is almost impossible on a slow table.

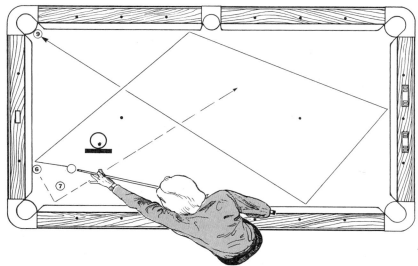

56 Four rails with draw

This four-railer is easier than the previous one because it's easy to get a thin hit without worrying about a kiss off the first rail. Again, you have to hit close to the side pocket without scratching. The dashed line describes the path of the 6-ball and emphasizes how thin the hit is. Here it is almost mandatory to use low English to make sure that the cueball doesn't curve on its way to the second rail. Because the 9-ball is hanging, safety plays here are dangerous. I'd go for the four-railer. Strike it with authority.

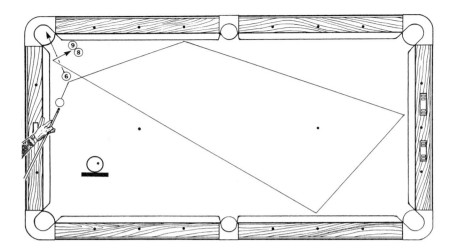

57 Four-rail breakout

In this position, it might be possible to carom the 6-ball into the pocket off the 8-ball without getting kissed out by the 9-ball. A slight change in the position rules out that approach. While it may seem impractical, cutting the 6-ball into the pocket and sending the cueball four rails to break open the cluster is not that difficult. This is one of those shots that an experienced three-cushion player can make almost every time.

You don't need a billiard table to practice billiard shots.

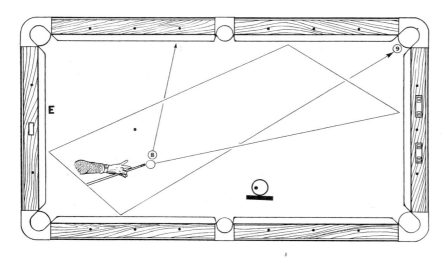

58 Another four-railer

This four-railer is not too tough provided you can hit the 8-ball extremely thin, so thin that the 8-ball just barely reaches the upper long rail. A thicker hit takes too much speed off the cueball. A lot of left English is required. If you think it's too tough, shoot softly and leave the cueball against the right short rail and defy your opponent to make a long cut shot.

Worth considering is shooting in the opposite direction, barely touching the 8-ball and hitting the first rail at point *E* for a one-rail bank to the 9-ball. Which shot is best depends on the exact position of the balls.

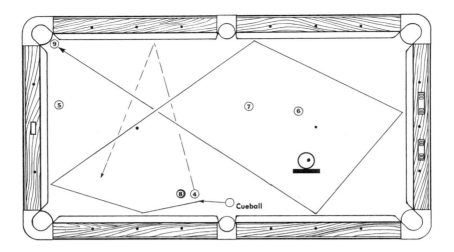

59 Standard five-railer

I call this five-rail shot "standard" because it comes up frequently in the game of three-cushion billiards and is considered fairly easy. It doesn't come up often in eight-ball or nine-ball because of interfering balls. Even when the path isn't blocked, a pool player might overlook the pattern. A very thin hit on the first ball is needed, especially on a slow table. It's not fairly easy if you've never practiced it.

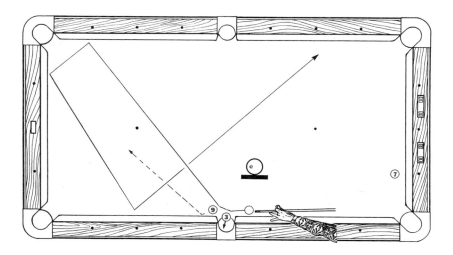

60 Second-ball position, outside

Diagrammed is a position in a game of nine-ball. The challenge is to run out. One avenue is to hit the 3-ball as thin as you can and draw the cueball to the upper long rail, leaving a cut on the 7-ball. This option is not too appetizing with the 9-ball in an unfavorable spot. There's a more crowd-pleasing way: Hit the 3-ball with left English so that the cueball caroms off the 9-ball as shown. The running English will carry the cueball around the table for position, while the 9-ball is bumped to a better place. Your opponent will be forced to concede that you are a hell of a player.

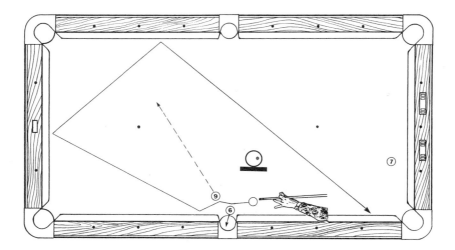

61 Second-ball position, inside

Here's another example of using a second ball to direct the cueball along a favorable path. In the diagram, making the 6-ball and getting position on the 7-ball isn't easy because the 9-ball is in the way. If the position is such that you can hit both balls thin, the three- or four-rail pattern is feasible.

Eine wichtige Frage beim Billardspiel.
Originalzeichnung von Georg Graf.

Are they touching? Maybe a flashlight will help.

Courtesy Heinrich Weingartner, Weingartner Museum of Billiards

When a cueball ball hits a motionless object ball, common sense tells you that the object ball will be propelled by the collision along a line directly opposite the contact point. Putting it another way, the object ball will be driven along the line formed by the line of centers of the two balls at impact. That is true only when there is no rubbing of the ball surfaces during the millisecond they are touching. If the surface of the cueball rubs against the surface of the object ball in a sideways direction, friction will throw the ball off line. The result is quite surprising to those who have never seen the effect demonstrated.

An object ball will be thrown off line by a cueball with sidespin or by a cueball that strikes it at an angle. A cut-shot exception is when there is just enough outside English on the cueball (right English if the object ball is being cut to the left) to make the leading edge of cueball roll off the surface of the object ball with no rubbing. The throw effect must be taken into consideration on every shot. A straight-in shot, for example, might be missed if sidespin is used. Fairly easy cut shots are sometimes missed because the frictional force at impact has the same effect as hitting the ball too full.

Fifteen pages are devoted to throw in *Byrne's New Standard Book of Pool and Billiards* and ten pages in *Byrne's Advanced Technique in Pool and Billiards* because unless you recognize throw and understand it, you will be a beginner forever. Throw shots are demonstrated on volume 1 of my video series.

How much a ball can be thrown off line depends on the condition of the balls. The effect is small with new or polished balls.

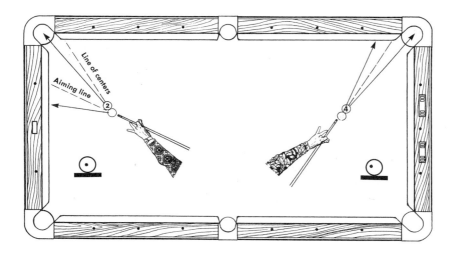

62 **Frozen cueball basics**

At the left is an example of direction-induced throw. The line of centers of the combination extends to the right side of the pocket. By aiming as shown, the friction between the balls causes the 2-ball to be thrown to the left into the pocket.

English-induced throw can be seen at the right. Even though the cue is aimed straight into the line of centers, the 4-ball can be thrown to the right and into the pocket with left English on the cueball.

Which of the two methods of throwing an object ball off line to choose depends on where you want the cueball to go. A few practice shots at various speeds is all you need to get the hang of it.

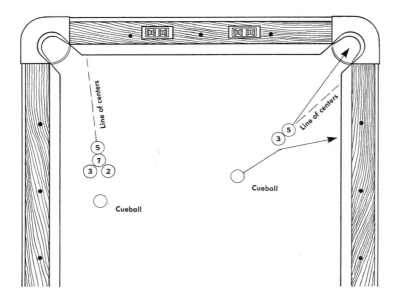

63 Combination basics

At the right is a frozen combination that isn't aimed at the pocket. To redirect the 5-ball to the left, hit the 3-ball on the right side. This is surprising news to beginners, even if they have college degrees in science. If the gap between the balls is a half inch and the line of centers is the same, you would have to hit the 3-ball on the left side to cut the 5-ball in.

The point to remember is that the position of the third ball is what influences a combination that is frozen or almost frozen. At the left, hitting the 3-ball results in failure. Hitting the 2-ball first throws the 5-ball into the pocket.

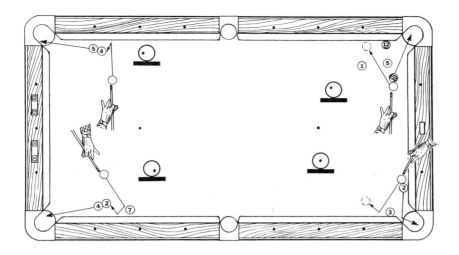

64 Four applications

Many frozen combinations are very easy provided you allow for the throw effect. By the same token, frozen combos that are straight in can be missed if the first ball is hit on one side or the other. At the upper left, you'll miss if you shoot straight at the 4-ball; coming off the rail is the key. At the lower left, the 4-ball can be made only if the 2-ball is hit on the side closest to the cushion, which is possible thanks to the position of the 7-ball.

At the upper right is a scene from a game of eight-ball. To make the 10-ball and get position on the 12-ball, shoot softly and throw the 10-ball into the pocket with left English. At the lower right, the way to make the 2-ball and get position on the 3-ball is to use no English and angle the cue as shown.

Understanding throw makes these four shots simple.

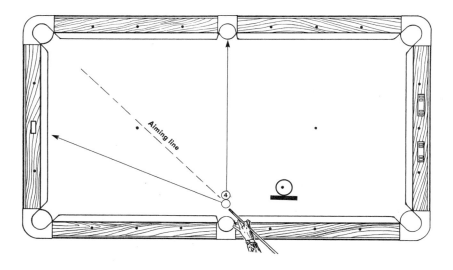

65 The roll-off shot

The cueball is frozen to the 4-ball and they are aimed straight at the side pocket. Can the 4-ball be made in the side and the cueball sent to the left short rail? Yes, and the method is known to hardly anybody. The secret is to use a little left English, which tends to throw the 4-ball to the right, while aiming to the left, which tends to throw the 4-ball to the left. Thus the forces cancel each other. The shot can be made no matter what the angle of aim and at any speed if the English is adjusted to prevent the ball surfaces from rubbing together. The thinner you aim, the more English you must apply.

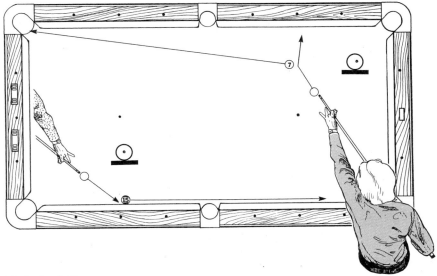

66 Cut-shot throw

For years, most players didn't think that the throw effect occurred on cut shots, and there are a few who still don't think so. It's easy to see throw when two balls are frozen, because the direction of the line of centers is obvious. On a cut shot with the balls separated by more than, say, an inch, the human eye can't determine the exact line of centers at the moment of impact. The frictional force is there in any case and must be taken into account. What that means is that on a cut shot, you must hit the object ball a hair thinner than the geometry suggests, unless, as already explained, outside English is used to keep the surface of the cueball from rubbing against the object ball.

That throw occurs on cut shots can be proved by an experiment you can try yourself. See *Byrne's Advanced Technique* (1990), page 25.

Try the cut shot at the right in the above diagram with left and right English to see the change in the required contact point.

To run a ball frozen to the rail past the side pocket (bottom of diagram) is very nearly impossible without hitting the rail first or using outside (right) English. Hit the rail first and the cueball sinks into the rail enough to make the line of centers diverge from the rail, permitting throw to keep the 15-ball on the rail. You'll never make it hitting the cueball in the center and hitting the rail and the ball at the same time.

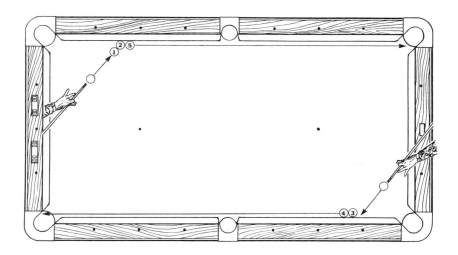

67 Frozen rail combos

At the bottom, you can't make the 4-ball if you hit the 3-ball full in the face because friction at the contact point will throw the 4-ball into the rail. You must hit the 3-ball thinly.

At the top is a beloved hustler's trick. If the three balls are frozen, the 5-ball won't go in unless the contact point between the 2-ball and the 5-ball is moistened with saliva, which greatly reduces the friction. Look closely, however, and you'll see that in the diagram there is a gap between the 2 and the 5. If the gap is roughly the thickness of three credit cards, the 5-ball will stay on the rail and go into the corner pocket.

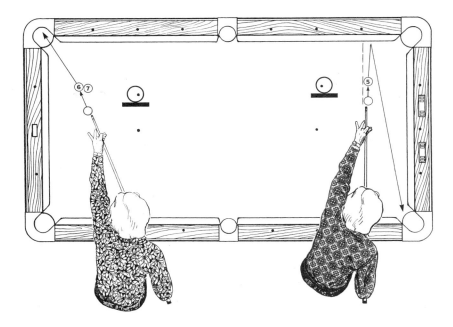

68 Two crucial shots

At the left is a position that comes up frequently. You must hit the 6-ball first, but the 7-ball is obscuring the point on the 6-ball that is directly opposite the pocket. The 6-ball can be thrown to the left with heavy right English. It's up to you to decide under game conditions whether it can be thrown enough.

By the way, your attempt to hit as much of the 6-ball as possible might result in hitting the 7-ball first, which is a foul. Split hits, where it is impossible to tell which ball was hit first, are ruled in favor of the shooter.

Throw can have a big effect on bank shots because the object ball can be thrown off line and given a slight sideways rotation. At the right, the dashed line is drawn one diamond from the end rail. Set up two balls as shown and shoot straight at the 5-ball. Unless the balls are extremely clean, you should be able to bank the 5 without allowing the cueball to drift more than a couple of inches left of the line.

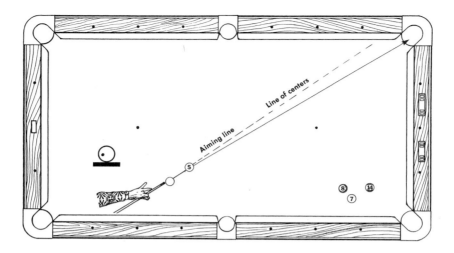

69 Minimizing drift

In a game of eight-ball, you have the solids and are faced with a long shot on the 5-ball that isn't quite straight in, as you can see from the dashed line of centers. If you cut it in with no English, the cueball might drift too far to the left and leave you with no way to make the 7-ball. By cutting the 5 only slightly, however, using left English, you can throw it to the right while holding the cueball to a leftward drift of less than an inch.

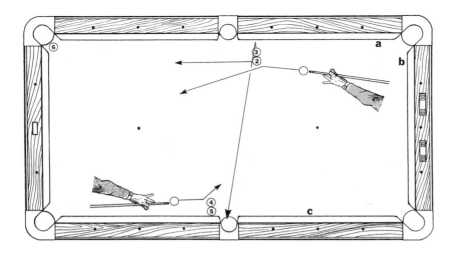

70 Two throw banks

At the top of the diagram, the 2-ball and the 3-ball are lined up at a right angle to the rail. Struck as shown, the 3-ball will bank into the side because the 2-ball not only sends it into the rail at a slight angle but also imparts a little sidespin.

The same principle is used in the well-known trick shot at the bottom. The two balls are perpendicular to the rail, several inches from the side pocket, and frozen to each other and the rail. Striking the cueball as shown will send the 4-ball into the lower-right corner pocket while the 5-ball is given enough side-spin to bank into the upper side pocket. The cueball, with right English hits *a, b,* and *c* and pockets the 6-ball in the upper-left corner pocket. The shot looks good and is not terribly difficult.

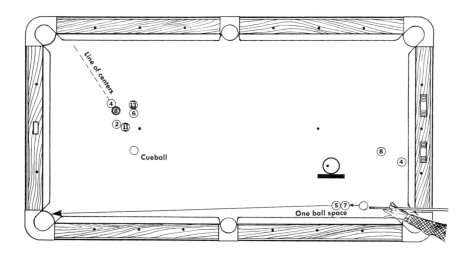

71 Two puzzles

At the left is a cluster of balls in a game of eight-ball. You have the solids. Can you make a ball? Don't look at the next sentence if you want to figure it out for yourself. The solution lies in hitting the right side of the 6-ball. The 6-ball caroms into the right side of the 8-ball, which throws the 4-ball to the left and into the corner.

The two-ball combination at the lower right was shown to me by John Fullerton. To throw a single ball to the left, right English is required. If there are two frozen balls as shown, use left English. The balls will act enough like interlocking gears to throw the 5-ball toward the rail and into the pocket.

SIDESPIN 6

Postcard, circa 1910, one of several thousand on billiard themes.

Bamford & Co., Ltd., Publishers

When the margin of error is small—on a long shot, for example, or when part of the intended pocket is blocked—forget about using sidespin (English). Hitting the cueball anywhere but on the vertical axis introduces three factors that make precision aiming difficult. Unless the cue is perfectly level, sidespin will make the cueball curve (the massé effect) on its way to the object ball. Sidespin causes "squirt," also called "deflection," terms used to describe the way the cueball's path diverges from the aiming line formed by the axis of the cue. Finally, sidespin on the cueball will throw the object ball off line, as we have seen in the previous section.

If the cue is only slightly elevated, as it is for most shots, and if you use only a little sidespin, then the effect on aiming is usually not important. Heavy sidespin, though, affects the cueball and the object ball so much that you should restrict its use to shots with a generous margin of error.

Contrary to widespread opinion, horizontal sidespin on the cueball does not make it curve. To prove this, spin a ball in place like a top, then roll another ball into it. The spinning ball will travel down the table in a straight line even though it is spinning at high speed. Curve occurs only when the cueball is struck a downward blow.

Another factoid: Only about 2 percent of the cueball's spin can be transferred to an object ball (the exact amount depends on how dirty the balls are), but that is enough to turn success into failure on many shots, especially banks.

When hitting the cueball off center, the maximum effect is achieved when the tip hits the ball halfway from the center to the edge; beyond that is a sure miscue. Risking a miscue by hitting the cueball that far from the center is rarely necessary.

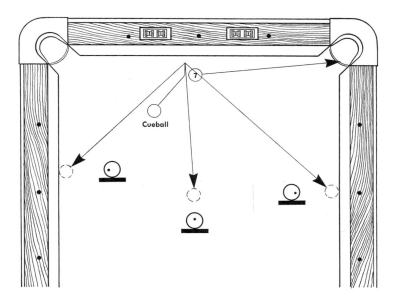

72 Sidespin limits

Place the balls exactly as shown and see if you can duplicate the cueball paths. In each case, hit the 7-ball just hard enough to make it in the corner. At the left, compensate for throw by hitting the 7-ball a hair thicker than you would with no English. To make the cueball travel to the second diamond on the right rail, compensate for throw by hitting the 7-ball a hair thinner than you would with no English.

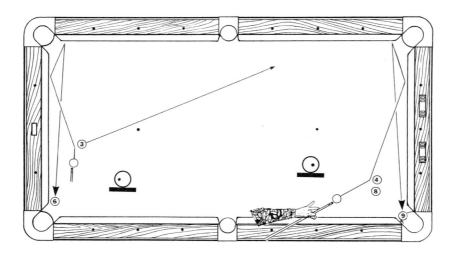

73 Double the rail

The two shots shown here are common in three-cushion billiards but not often seen in pool. Many players are unfamiliar with this pattern or are not confident enough to try it. At the left, a blocker ball might prevent a straight draw from the 3-ball to the 6-ball, or you might want to drive the 3-ball into a cluster to break it up. The 3-ball is three ball spaces from the left rail. Hit as little 3-ball as possible without sending the cueball into the pocket points.

At the right, the 4-ball is three ball spaces from the rail. Don't hit the cueball above center, because follow will cause the cueball to bend toward the rail, creating a more difficult double-the-rail angle than is necessary. Instead, use stun action (neither follow nor draw) so that the cueball travels in a straight line to the first rail.

Shots like these impress spectators at tournaments, even though they aren't particularly difficult for skilled players.

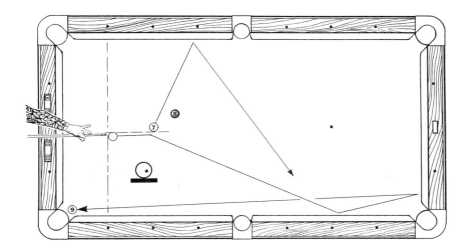

74 Doubling the long way

This is harder than the previous two shots because the distances are greater and the margin of error is smaller. To practice the diagrammed shot, place the 7-ball on the head spot and the cueball exactly as shown, with its left edge even with the right edge of the 7-ball. On my table, this position is near the limit for double-the-rail action. Hit the cueball on the equator (neither above nor below center) with maximum right English.

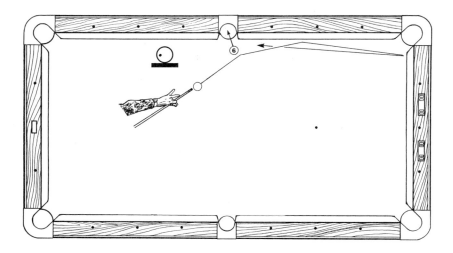

75 Doubling for position

Opportunities sometimes arise to use double-the-rail action for positioning the cueball. Cutting a ball into the side with inside English, as shown in the diagram, is an example. The maneuver is sometimes useful in straight pool to get a favorable angle on a break ball.

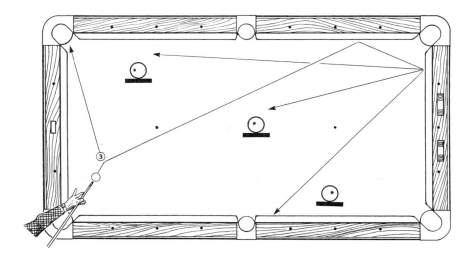

76 Sidespin effects

Sidespin doesn't have a great effect on how a cueball caroms off an object ball, but it dramatically changes the way the cueball rebounds from a cushion. In the diagram, look at the way the cueball path off the second rail is affected by the English. The examples show what happens with heavy left, slight left, and running (right). You must be able to approximate these results to consider yourself a good player.

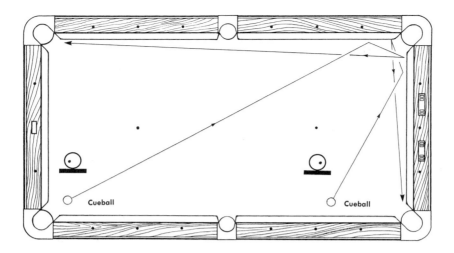

77 Doubling limits

This is the best I can do on my table. At the right, shooting the cueball from the second diamond, I can just barely get back to the end rail off the side rail. At the lower left, the angle into the first rail is the same. There is a knack to getting this much cueball action. Hit the cueball a little below center and don't shoot hard. Developing good judgment on double-the-rail patterns will add a new dimension to your position game and enable you to escape from many seemingly impossible safeties.

The limits suggested in the diagram can be exceeded if the cueball goes off a ball into the rail because the carom removes some of the cueball's speed but very little of its spin.

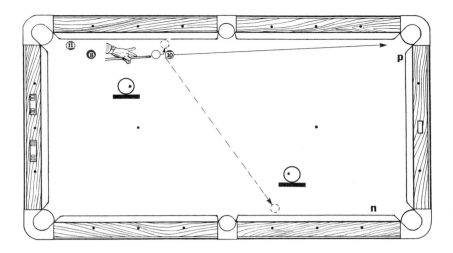

78 The "impossible" position shot

Generally speaking, you can't cut a ball to the left and make the cueball go to the left as well without resorting to a chancy massé. An exception is diagrammed. The cueball is within one ball space of the 10-ball and both are one ball width from the rail. Let's say you want to make the 10-ball in the corner and leave the cueball closer to the rail than it is now for a shot at the 11-ball. The trick is to aim as if you were cutting the 10-ball slightly *away* from the pocket, toward point *p,* and use heavy right sidespin. Unless the balls are extremely slippery, it's possible to throw the ball into the pocket and leave the cueball on or near the rail.

Interestingly, from the same position you can make the 10-ball and send the cueball all the way across the table as denoted by the dashed line. To do that, aim at point *n* with left sidespin. At first glance, it doesn't appear that the layout offers so much positional freedom.

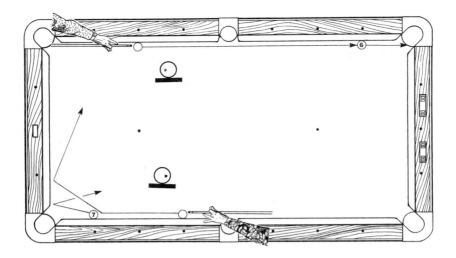

79 Inside and outside sidespin

It is well known among the pool cognoscenti that the position at the top of the diagram presents little difficulty. The cueball and the 6-ball are frozen to the rail, but the shot can be made with left English. The cueball leaves the rail just enough to eliminate the risk of hitting a side-pocket point, then curves back in (because the cue is slightly elevated so the butt can clear the left short rail) to make the 6-ball. Shoot softly to avoid following the ball into the pocket, or use some low English and shoot hard enough to stop the cueball on impact.

Why, I asked myself for decades, is the same shot impossible with outside English? Even when only two diamonds separate the balls, as is the case at the bottom of the diagram, the object ball can't be made if you use right-hand English. Is it because squirt sends the cueball into the rail and out again? Then there ought to be a line of aim that compensates for that, but hundreds of trials over the years have failed to uncover it. Try this shot and convince yourself of its impossibility before turning to the next diagram, where the secret of making it is revealed.

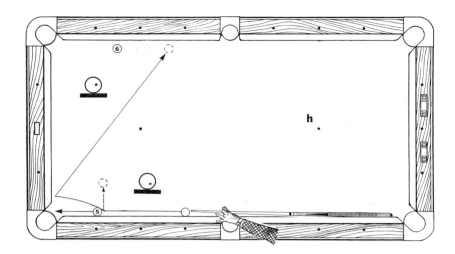

80 A rail-shot trick

When I asked Bob Jewett, my technical consultant, why the frozen rail shot can't be made with outside English, he suggested that the reason may be that the edge of the cueball is under the nose of the cushion. A cueball frozen to a rail can't be made to stay on the rail if it is struck with an elevated cue, because it can't jump freely. (See "Jewett's rail draw trap" in *Byrne's Treasury of Trick Shots* [1982], page 160.) On the great majority of shots, the cue is not quite level when the tip hits the cueball; even if the elevation is slight, the cueball will be forced away from the rail by the cushion nose. A further problem is that outside English with a cue that is even slightly elevated will make the cueball curve in the direction of the English—that is, away from the frozen object ball. A cueball will curve to the left with right English only if you are shooting up at it, which can be shown by resting the cueball on a stack of chalk cubes on a rail and shooting up at it from a kneeling position.

Happily, the diagrammed shot can be made, but not every time. The secret is to shoot up at the cueball. You don't have to remove the end rail to do it; with the cueball positioned at the third diamond, the butt of the cue clears the end rail on a nine-foot table. Rest the butt on the cloth and push it under the rail. The stroke is awkward because you can't encircle the cue with your fingers—the butt must stay in contact with the bed of the table and the underside of the cushion. Hit the cueball with just a little right English. The angle of the cue compensates for squirt, and the upward tilt of the cue makes the cueball curve just a hair left. I have managed to send the cueball to the opposite side of the table with right follow and to send it straight out from the rail with stun. On one happy occasion, follow sent the cueball all the way to point *h*.

A shot like this may never come up in one of your games. It is presented here in the spirit of pure scientific inquiry and as a gambling proposition. See it demonstrated on my *Gamebreakers* video.

"That's not a foul, is it?"

Courtesy Heinrich Weingartner, Weingartner Museum of Billiards

Topspin, or follow, is the most common type of cueball rotation because it's what you get when you simply roll a ball down the table. Natural roll, in which there is no slippage between the ball and the cloth, is, believe it or not, the most topspin you can put on a cueball when you shoot it down the table.

Hit a cueball in the center and it will slide for a short distance before the friction of the cloth converts the slide into natural roll. To give the cueball natural roll from the moment it is struck, the tip of the cue must contact the cueball halfway from the center to the top. A higher hit means a miscue, consequently there is no way to put an excess of topspin on the cueball. As scientist George Onoda has helpfully pointed out, maximum backspin, sidespin, and topspin can be practiced by using a striped ball because the stripe is exactly half a ball wide. Clean a striped ball, chalk your tip so it will leave a mark on the ball, and convince yourself that halfway out from the center is as far as you can safely hit a cueball. In the diagram, note that the bottom edge of the tip hits the top edge of stripe.

81 Topspin limit

Unfortunately for this particular practice method, some balls now have a stripe that is wider than half a ball.

There is no technical difference between the terms "follow" and "force follow." The latter is used when the cueball is struck hard, and almost all players think that by using high speed they are spinning the cueball faster than natural roll, but such is not the case. The rotational speed is greater on a high-speed follow shot only because the linear speed is greater. Until the cueball hits a ball, there is no slippage between the cueball and the cloth.

When a cueball with natural roll hits an object ball full, it stops dead if the balls are the same weight, but the cueball doesn't stop spinning. Because of the friction of the cloth, the topspin quickly makes the cueball resume its forward roll. Watch for it and you will see the hesitation on a full-hit follow shot.

With those points in mind, let's look at some follow shots.

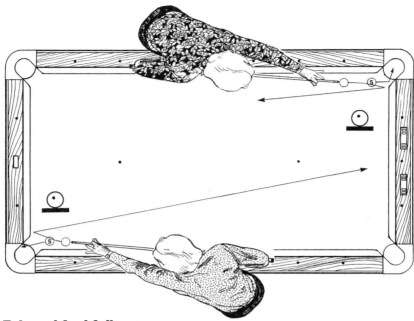

82 Fair and foul follows

Once you and the world's referees understand that when a cueball with follow hits an object ball full it hesitates before following, it is easy to recognize the small-gap foul. As explained in Section 2, the shot at the bottom of the diagram is a foul if the cue follows through to hit the cueball again. The double hit makes it easy to bank the cueball to the other end of the table for position. If the cueball doesn't hesitate at impact, the stroke is a foul. With such evidence at hand, there should be no cause for arguments.

To see the difference between fair and foul, set up the shot shown at the top right, with six inches between the balls. Use maximum follow, shoot hard, and note the hesitation of the cueball. It's not easy to get the cueball to the other end of the table with topspin alone. The cueball might still have topspin when it comes off the rail, which will kill its speed completely.

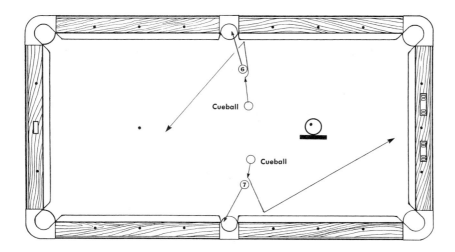

83 Cheating the pocket

The two positions diagrammed here are identical and are designed to illustrate what can be done to control the cueball by combining topspin, sidespin, and cheating the pocket.

At the top, by using high left English and hitting the 6-ball as fully as possible, the cueball can be made to follow the indicated path. Use minimum speed so that the cueball doesn't jump too far to the right before curving forward.

At the bottom, a completely different cueball path results when the cueball is struck with high left and the 7-ball is driven into the far side of the pocket.

The longer the shot, of course, the riskier it is to try to drive a ball into one side of a pocket or the other.

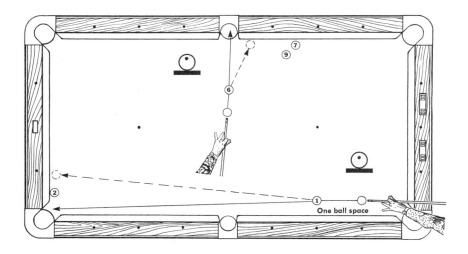

84 Speed control

It is easier to judge the length of a full-hit follow shot than a draw shot. Let's say you have ball in hand and are facing the position at the top of the diagram in a game of nine-ball. Considerable precision is needed to pocket the 6-ball and get position on the 7-ball. One choice you have (not shown here) is to place the cueball between the 6-ball and the upper side pocket with the intention of making the 6-ball in the lower side pocket and drawing back to the rail for shape on the 7-ball. When close control of the cueball is required, the diagrammed follow shot is the best bet.

To drive home the point that follow is easier to control than draw, set up the position at the bottom of the diagram. The cueball and the 1-ball are each one ball space from the rail. The challenge is to make the 1-ball and leave the cueball within a few inches of the left end rail for position on the 2-ball. A good player can do it consistently. Judging a six-foot draw shot with the same degree of accuracy is far more difficult.

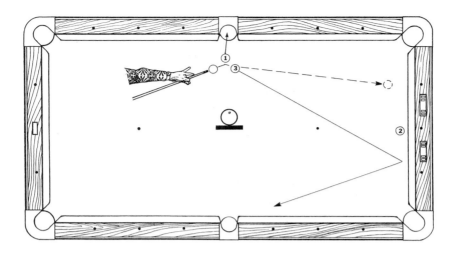

85 Second-ball follow

The problem here is to make the 1-ball and get position on the 2-ball. This would stump a lot of players, but the solution is quite simple. Use topspin and adjust the hit on the 1-ball (the margin of error is huge) so that the cueball makes a full hit on the 3-ball. The topspin will still be there, and the cueball will proceed like magic to the right end of the table. There is something satisfying about the action and the way the blocker ball turns out to be no obstacle at all. Try it; you'll like it.

NOTE: This idea can be used defensively if the cueball is close to two balls near an end rail. Hitting the first ball thin moves it only a little, while the cueball follows through the second ball to the other end of the table.

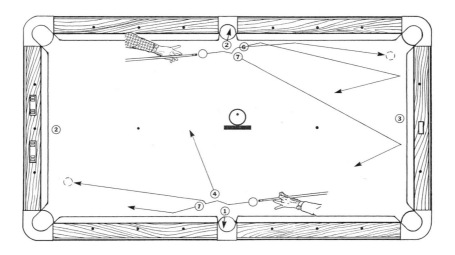

86 Third-ball follow

These two positions from games of nine-ball (the lowest ball must be struck first) are similar in that two balls block the cueball's path. If you can cut the first ball so that the cueball will carom thinly off a second ball into a third ball, then top-spin will carry the cueball to the far end of the table. Remember that the cueball will lose speed caroming off a second ball, so shoot harder than required in the previous example.

It is very difficult to hit the third ball exactly where you want to when the cueball caroms off two balls instead of one, even when the cluster is as tight as the one at the top of the diagram. The cueball will follow forward, but the path is impossible to predict with accuracy.

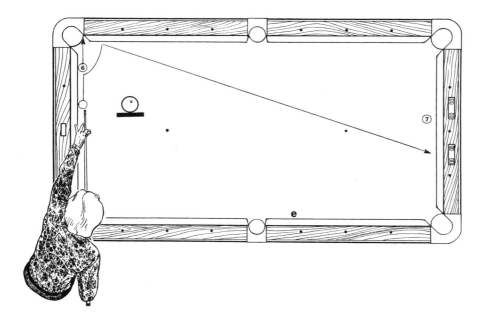

87 Frozen surprise

A frozen surprise is not a dessert; it's what I call a method of sending a cueball the length of the table when it is frozen to an end rail along with the object ball. You'll have to admit that the diagrammed position is unpromising. The cueball and the 6-ball are straight in and frozen to the rail, while the next ball to be pocketed is at the other end. Position on the 7-ball is possible because the 6-ball is close enough to the corner pocket to provide a sufficient margin of error—that is, it doesn't have to be driven straight in.

Line the shot up with the cue parallel to the rail. Use high right English and shoot hard, and the cueball will follow a path close to the one diagrammed while spinning like a top. I call it a surprise because that's what I felt, along with joy, when I discovered this shot while practicing in June of 2002.

NOTE: With less right sidespin, the cueball can be sent to the area around point *e*.

The similar shot in the last diagram of the previous section is impossible with outside English because the balls are farther apart and farther from the pocket, eliminating the margin of error.

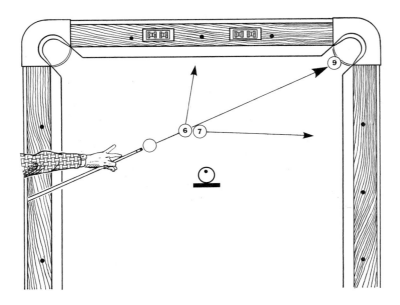

88 Clearance follow

Shots of this type go unnoticed even in games between very good players. Playing safe by hitting the 6-ball thin on the right edge with right sidespin is not a bad idea, but if your opponent can see any part of the 6-ball when she comes to the table, she might be able to find a way to make the jawed 9-ball.

Even though the 6-7 combination is not aimed at anything useful, it is easy to contact the 6-ball first and make the 9-ball. Hit the 6-ball full in the face with topspin; the 6 and 7 will get out of the way and the cueball will continue forward to make the 9-ball. Slow speed is prudent here to avoid following the 9-ball into the corner for a scratch.

Easy clearance shots like this don't come up often, but when they do, it's a shame to overlook them. Keep your eyes peeled.

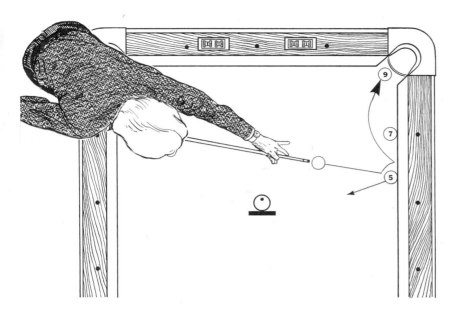

89 Rail curve

You'll lose a customer if you make this force-back-to-the-rail shot in a money game. Hit the 5-ball very full—how full depends on the exact angle of approach—shoot hard, use maximum follow, and you at least have a chance of seeing the cueball bend around the 7-ball to pocket the 9-ball. It's not a shot you will make the first time you try it. In a tournament or money game, it would probably be wiser to play safe than to miss and sell out, but in a pastime game, I would go for it and try to be a hero.

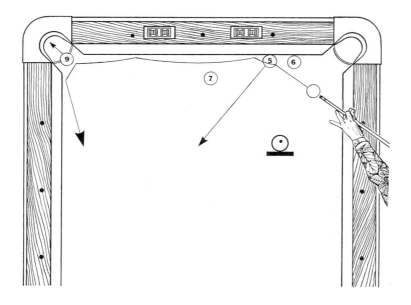

90 Phelan's follow

Here's another shot that you'll see tried more often in an exhibition of trick shots than in an important game, but the concept is worth knowing. It's a common pattern in three-cushion billiards.

The 5-ball is frozen to the rail—if it isn't, the action is much harder to achieve. Use maximum topspin on the cueball and hit the 5-ball directly in the center. Cutting the 5-ball even a hair to the right or left ruins your chances of forcing the cueball to stay on the rail or curve back to the rail to pocket the jawed ball.

The shot was known 150 years ago and was discussed by Michael Phelan in his 1857 book *The Game of Billiards.* (See *Byrne's Treasury of Trick Shots in Pool and Billiards* [1982], page 35.) In Phelan's version, the 5-ball was sent four rails around the table to go into the same pocket as the 9-ball. Those old-timers were *good*!

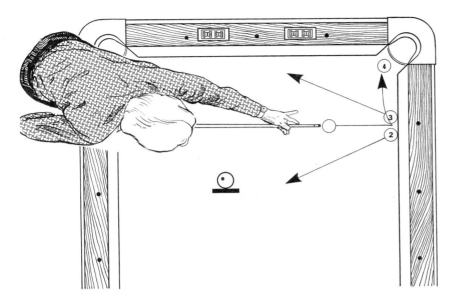

91 McCleery's creep

I found this interesting item in Professor J. F. B. McCleery's 1890 book *The Mc-Cleery Method of Billiard Playing.* He called it "the creep shot" and played it with the cueball eight feet from the object balls. The 2-ball and the 3-ball should be about an inch and a quarter apart (the diagonal of a chalk cube). Use high left and shoot hard. On new cloth it's possible to make the cueball go back to the rail twice before pocketing the jawed ball.

It doesn't seem to make any difference which ball you hit first, but the professor recommends the ball farthest from the target—the 2-ball in this case. A split hit also works.

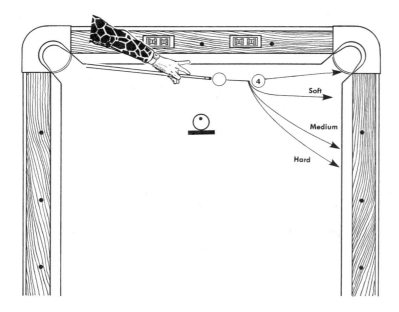

92 Cut-shot follow

When a rolling cueball hits an object ball at an angle, it caroms off the ball at right angles to the path of the object ball and then bends forward. Of theoretical interest is the fact that the curve is a parabola, of practical interest is that the sharpness of the curve depends on the cueball's speed. The curves are approximated in the diagram and demonstrated on *Byrne's Standard Video of Pool, Volume II.* The player who has the knowledge, skill, and touch to envision the curves accurately has a big advantage.

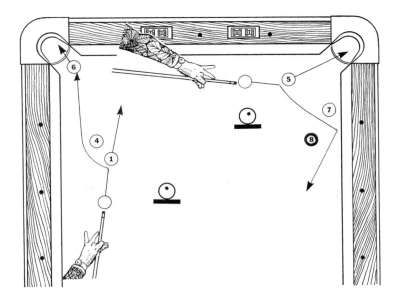

93 Applying the curve

At the left is one way to take advantage of the way the cueball curves on an angled follow shot. Hit the 1-ball just a little to the left of dead center with a hard stroke and high follow. With a little luck and a lot of talent, you can make the cueball bend around the obstacle to make the 6-ball.

At the right, the problem is to make the 5-ball and get the cueball to the other end of the table. By choosing the right speed, you can send the cueball through the hole. Shoot too hard and the cueball hits the 8-ball, too soft and the 7-ball is in the way.

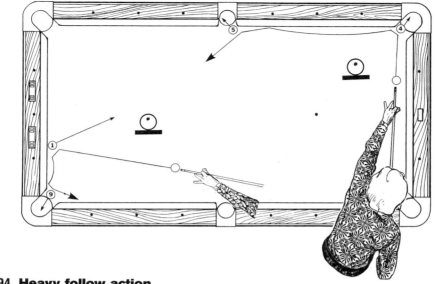

94 Heavy follow action

On page 106 I mentioned that a cueball's speed will be killed if it still has forward topspin when it bounces off a rail. That behavior can be exploited. At the lower left of the diagram is a position from a game of nine-ball. What's the best way to make the hanging 9-ball? If the 1-ball is a half inch or more from the rail, draw is the best idea. But if the 1-ball is frozen or close to being frozen, follow is a tempting alternative. Beginners sometimes get this hug-the-rail action by accident. With good players, it's no accident.

At the top of the diagram, balls are perched on the lips of two pockets. Rarely under game conditions is trying to make two balls at once a good idea, so the diagrammed shot is presented for your amusement only. Hit the 4-ball full and hard with follow and see if you can bend back to the rail to make the 5-ball as well. Exhibition players sometimes go a step further and try to carom the cueball off the 5-ball into a ball in the jaws of the pocket in the lower-left corner. Making three balls in such a fashion is about a one-in-ten proposition even for an expert.

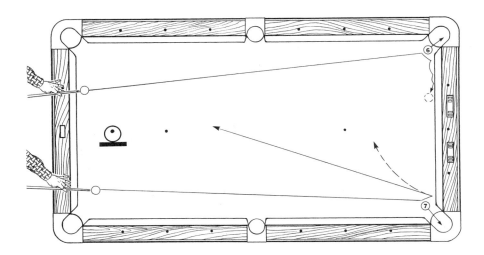

95 A treacherous shot

At the bottom, the player wants to make the 7-ball and return the cueball to the other end of the table. It looks easy, but if the 7-ball is hit a little too full, the topspin on the cueball will bend its path toward the upper rail, as shown by the dashed line. You must hit the 7-ball so thin that the rebound speed off the rail overwhelms the topspin. On a thick hit, so much linear speed is taken off the cueball that the topspin predominates.

On the other hand, you might want the topspin to rule, as in the shot at the top. To keep the cueball near the right end rail, you can either shoot very softly and risk missing the 6-ball by having the cueball roll off line, or hit it hard and let the topspin do the work.

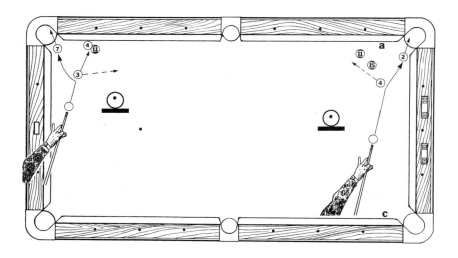

96 Thick or thin?

Over a wide range of angles, the cueball can be made to carom off an object ball and hit a target (a ball or a spot on a rail) with either a thick or a thin hit. Billiard players make the decision frequently in their efforts to play safe, play position, or miss a kiss.

At the left is a position from a game of rotation. The 7-ball can be made by hitting the left edge of the 3-ball, but the next shot won't be easy, and the 4-ball is still buried behind the 11-ball. Better is to hit the 3 full, driving it into the cluster and making the 7 as shown.

At the right, the game is eight-ball. Making the 2-ball by grazing the right edge of the 4-ball leaves no second shot. Better is to drive the 4-ball to point *a,* across the table to point *c,* and out to the middle of the table, while the cueball follows forward to make the 2. The full hit on the 4-ball will double bank it to a favorable position.

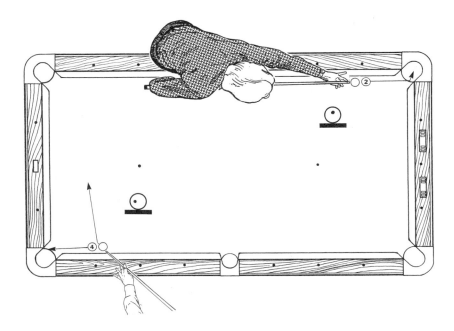

97 Small-gap follow

At the top, the gap between the balls is only a quarter of an inch. It takes very good cue control to apply follow with a level cue and avoid the foul. It is easy to imagine a situation like this in which you must make the 2-ball and move the cueball forward a few inches. The best way to avoid the foul with a level cue is to reduce the bridge to a minimum, that is, move your bridge hand as close as possible to the cueball. Restricting the room for a normal backstroke makes it easier to restrict the follow-through. Hit the cueball very high and softly and it will follow a few inches. It may also help you to use an open bridge so you can lift the tip at the instant of impact instead of following through.

Another method of getting some topspin on the cueball without hitting it twice is to elevate the cue to about a 45-degree angle and aim slightly above the center of mass of the cueball. Aim so that the axis of the cue is directed through the cueball to the near edge of the object ball. (If the cueball were a hollow bubble and all of its weight were concentrated in a steel ball bearing at its exact center, the ball bearing would be the center of mass. To impart topspin, the axis of the cue must pass above it.)

If topspin is not essential for position, then the shot should be handled as shown at the lower left—a thin hit with inside English to avoid the double hit.

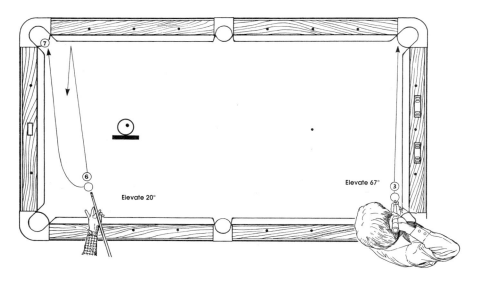

98 Massé follow and draw

At the left, the gap is about half an inch. With a cue elevated about 20 degrees, and right follow on the cueball, the cueball path can be made to curve as shown. The right English helps avoid the kiss as the cueball caroms to the left off the 6-ball. Because the cueball only has to travel about four feet, soft speed will suffice.

At the right is another small-gap position. By elevating the cue to about 67 degrees, you can follow, stop, or draw the cueball. For follow, aim above the center of mass; for stop, aim directly at the center of mass; for draw, aim below the center of mass. If you are drawing the cueball, be sure to get the cue out of the way in time.

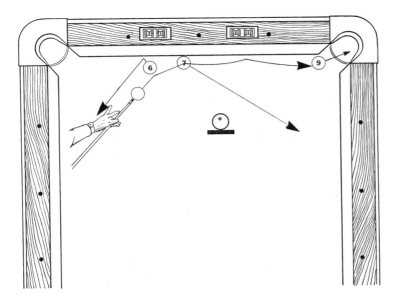

99 Phelan off a ball

In Diagram 90, the Phelan follow shot was described. The same hug-the-rail action can be achieved off a ball, as shown here. The cueball must have topspin and must hit the 7-ball squarely, not even a hair to the right or left of center.

Depending on the exact position of the balls, it might be easier to hit the 6-ball full on the right side and bend around the 7-ball to make the 9-ball.

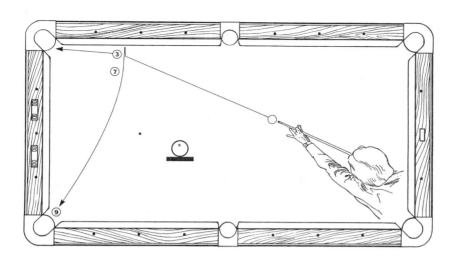

100 Cross-table dive

Not many pool players would see the opportunity to make the 9-ball in this position, where the 7-ball seems to be in the way. If the cueball has topspin, it is bound to bend forward. Judging the curve with accuracy isn't easy because it depends on the amount of topspin, the hit on the object ball, and the speed of the cueball. A good player will either make the 9-ball or come close almost every time.

Even when it is not possible to make the first object ball, the cross-table dive might still be the best chance to win the game.

Monks, circa 1875, practicing one of many meditation techniques.

Courtesy Heinrich Weingartner, Weingartner Museum of Billiards

Putting backspin on the cueball by hitting it below center makes possible some of the most beautiful shots in the game. While nonplayers may be intrigued to see a cueball back up after a collision in apparent defiance of the laws of physics, this shot is more than a curiosity for players. The player who can apply backspin, or draw the ball, with control has a powerful weapon on both offense and defense.

That so many players can't draw the ball even though they have been playing for years is one of the most lamentable aspects of the human condition. And yet the basic technique is not hard to learn. Advanced applications, of course, require a secure stroke, considerable practice, and that thing called talent.

In my experience as a teacher, students who can't draw the ball are almost always not hitting the cueball low enough. They are afraid of golfing the ball—perhaps sending it off the table or ripping the cloth—but that seldom happens if the tip of the cue is shaped properly and well chalked. The second-most common error is shooting too softly. Low speed is okay if the cueball is a foot or less away from the object ball, but as the distance between the balls increases, so must the speed. The friction between the cueball and the cloth is constantly acting to reduce the backspin and convert it into natural roll.

To learn how to hit the cueball low enough to get good draw action, use a striped ball as a cueball and orient the stripe horizontally (be sure that the stripe on the ball is no more than half a ball width for this exercise).

101 Backspin limit

In Diagram 101, note that the upper edge of the cue tip is contacting the lower edge of the stripe on a 9-ball—that's how you get maximum backspin. Any lower and you'll miscue, especially if the tip hits the cloth before the ball. Examine the 9-ball after shooting; the chalk mark made by the tip tells you if you hit the intended spot. When practicing, start with a short, straight-in shot and remember to get the cue out of the way of the returning cueball.

In the drawing, the cue is not quite level, which is the case when the butt must clear a rail. A slightly elevated cue, in fact, makes the draw action livelier. The disadvantage is that unless you hit the cueball precisely in the center you have squirt and curve to contend with. That's why most teachers advocate a level cue for draw shots. In addition, the more you elevate, the more awkward it is to stroke smoothly and the harder it is to judge speed. Except for certain trick shots, a level cue will produce enough draw for almost any situation.

For more coaching on draw shots, see *Byrne's Standard Video of Pool, Volume I.*

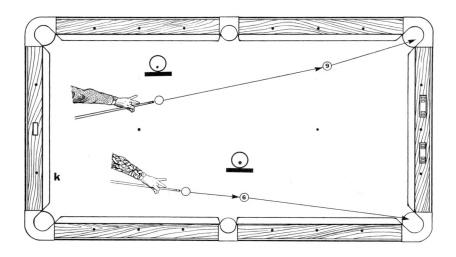

102 Two for starters

One application of backspin is to slow the cueball down on its way to a ball or a rail. At the top, for example, you might want to pocket the 9-ball and make the cueball follow a few inches. Instead of shooting very softly and taking the risk of the cueball rolling off line, you can add speed and use backspin. The goal is to let natural roll take over just before the cueball hits the 9-ball. A certain touch is required.

At the bottom is a practice shot that is simple but good. First, use backspin on the cueball and a slow speed that allows the backspin to disappear just at the moment of contact. The desired result is to stop the cueball dead—the so-called stop shot. Next use more speed—still hitting the cueball very low—so that the cueball comes back halfway to the starting point, then all the way back. Finally, see if you can draw the cueball all the way back to point *k* at the left end of the table, which doesn't take a forceful stroke if you hit the cueball low enough.

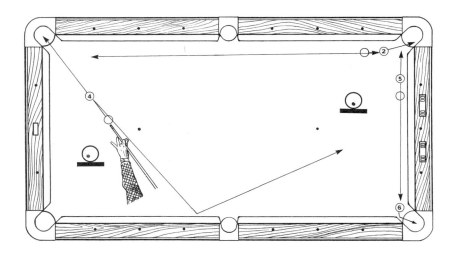

103 Three practice draws

At the right, place the cueball six inches from the 5-ball and see if you can make the 5 and draw back to make the 6-ball as well. In a game, however, there is very rarely a reason to make two balls at once, unless pocketing the second ball wins the game. It's almost always better to leave the second ball in the jaws so it can be used for position.

At the top right, the cueball is six inches from the 2-ball. Any good player can draw the cueball all the way to the other end of the table. Can you?

At the left is a severe challenge. The cueball is a foot from the 4-ball. The idea is to draw straight back using low left English and get the cueball to within a foot of the right end rail. It's not easy because adding sidespin means you can't hit the cueball quite as low. On the other hand, the sidespin gives the cueball a lively jump off the bottom long rail.

For all three shots, hit the cueball very low with a cue close to level and a well-chalked tip.

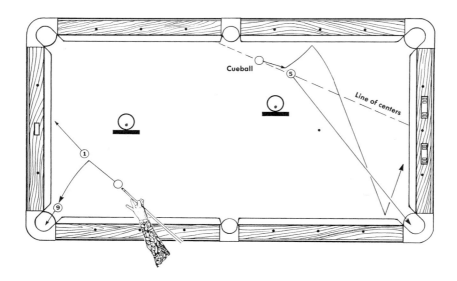

104 Two more tests

Shots like the one at the left come up frequently. The object is not to make the 1-ball, but rather to draw off the 1 to pocket a ball in the jaws. In the game of nine-ball, whenever the 9-ball comes to rest in or near the jaws, normal strategy goes out the window as the players try to find caroms and combinations to end the game without going to the bother of running the table.

How good is your draw stroke? To find out, set the cueball and the 5-ball a foot apart on a line connecting the middle diamond of the end rail with the corner of the side pocket as shown by the dashed line. See if you can make the 5-ball in the corner pocket and put enough draw on the cueball to make it follow a path close to the one in the diagram. Draw action like this comes in handy when playing position.

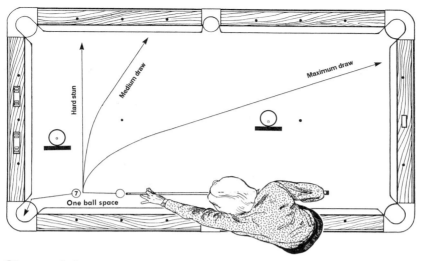

105 Stun and draw

The cueball and the 7-ball are one ball space from the rail and a foot apart. To send the cueball straight across the table, stun action is required, which is to say that the cueball must slide into the 7-ball. With only a foot separating the balls, the cueball will slide into the 7 without picking up significant topspin if it is hit in the center and hard. At greater distances, a below-center hit is needed.

Note the curves for medium and maximum draw. You need to be able to duplicate them for advanced position play. For more, see *Byrne's Standard Video of Pool, Volume II.*

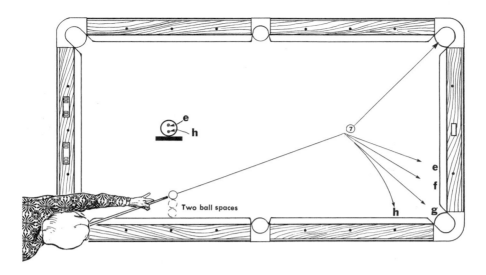

106 Spot-shot flexibility

The 7-ball is on the foot spot and the cueball is opposite the second diamond and two ball spaces off the rail. Hitting the cueball above center will send it to point *e* on the right end rail. The same path results if you hit the cueball in the center or even below center provided that you shoot softly enough for the backspin and slide to wear off and become natural roll by the time it hits the 7-ball.

Maximum draw bends the cueball path to point *h*. Less speed or less backspin sends the cueball to *f* and *g* or points in between. Top players show great skill in their use of less-than-maximum follow and draw.

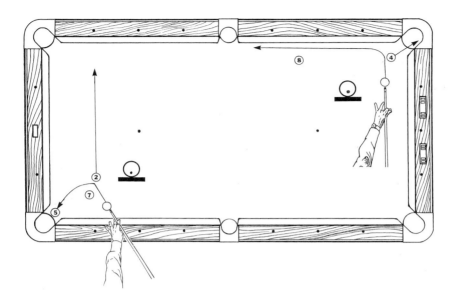

107 The curve-around draw

Here are two practical shots that make use of the curves shown in the previous diagrams. Examples could be multiplied endlessly. At the left, it's not difficult to hit the 2-ball and curve around the 7-ball to make the 5-ball. You have to be able to judge how hard to hit the 2-ball so that the cueball moves just far enough to the left before curving back. To acquire the knack, practice, practice, practice.

At the upper right, the player must make the 4-ball and make the cueball go through the hole between the 8-ball and the rail to get position on the next ball (which is omitted to simplify the diagram). Not difficult if you know how to blend the backspin, the speed, and the fullness of the hit.

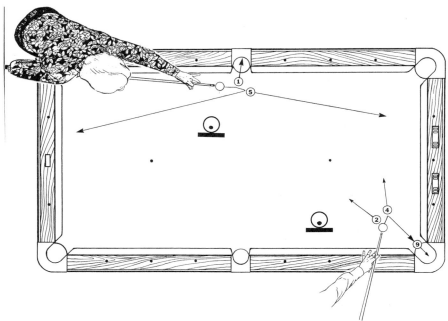

108 Second-ball draw

Just as the cueball can be made to follow through a second ball (see diagram 85 in the previous section), it can also be made to draw back from a second ball.

At the top, the player desires to make the 1-ball in the side and get the cueball to the left end rail for position. Would it occur to you to hit the cueball low and draw from the 5-ball? It's easy when the first ball is this close to the side, because the hit can be adjusted to make sure you hit the 5-ball squarely. The idea can also be used in safety play in a position where the first ball isn't next to a side pocket.

At the lower right is a position to die for in a game of nine-ball. Hit the 2-ball very thin and the draw action is the same as if you were hitting the 4-ball directly.

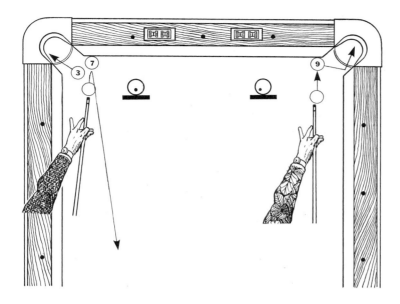

109 Frozen second-ball draw

Faced with the cozy position at the left, you can easily make the 3-ball and kiss back off the frozen 7-ball with backspin to the other end of the table. It's not really a draw shot, because a soft stroke is all that's needed to send the cueball nine feet. The double kiss is what makes the cueball reverse direction. Topspin spoils the action. The 7-ball doesn't have to be frozen to the rail, but if it is, it's easier to predict the cueball's path.

At the right, the 9-ball is so close to the pocket you might be able to take advantage of the generous margin of error. Hit the 9-ball squarely with low left and you have a chance of forcing it into the corner pocket because the 9-ball will pick up a little topspin from the backspin on the cueball. It's an easy shot on bar tables with cueballs heavier than the other balls. In the given position, it helps to be left-handed.

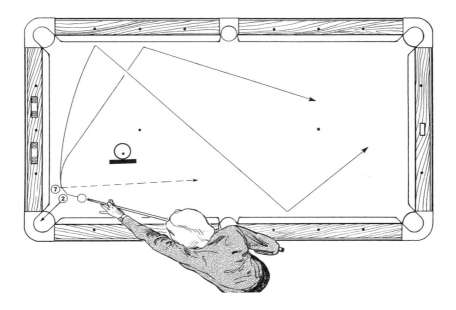

110 Angled second-ball draw

If the cueball hits the second ball at an angle, the result is much different from the previous diagram, where a double kiss is utilized. The two paths shown above depend on how thickly the cueball hits the 7-ball. While the paths are not exactly predictable, it is not difficult to at least get the cueball to the right end of the table.

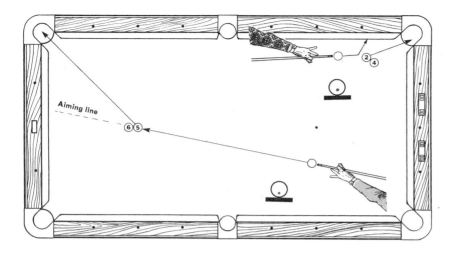

111 The frozen push-through

The coefficient of friction when one ball hits another is roughly 0.02, which means that about 2 percent of the cueball's spin can be transferred to an object ball. That frictional force is what makes sidespin throw possible. The slight turn given to the object ball by sidespin on the cueball is a significant factor on bank shots because it changes the rebound angle.

The two shots diagrammed depend in part on topspin being transferred to the object ball by a backspinning cueball. At the left, the 5-ball is on the head spot and the 6-ball is frozen to it. It is possible to force the 5-ball through the 6-ball and into the pocket by aiming as shown with a hard stroke and backspin on the cueball. It's fairly easy to get the 5-ball to move *toward* the corner pocket, but actually making it is no more than a one-in-five or one-in-ten chance even for a world-class player. I would play safe in this position unless I was sure my opponent couldn't run out if I missed the force-through.

The shot at the upper right is much easier because it is only necessary to force the 2-ball just a little forward of the tangent line and because the margin of error is large when the balls are this close to the pocket.

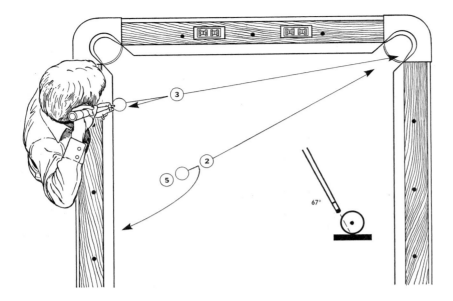

112 Elevated draw

It is possible to draw the cueball even when it is frozen to a rail or when another ball makes bridging awkward. In the two shots above, elevate your cue to about 67 degrees (halfway between 45 degrees and perpendicular). As shown in the inset, aim at the resting point of the cueball on the cloth, which as you can see is behind the center of mass of the cueball.

At the top, it's not so hard to get the cueball to draw back to the rail; what's hard is to make the 3-ball. When the distance from the cueball to the object ball is more than six or eight inches, the cueball must be struck exactly on the centerline, otherwise it will massé right or left. Aiming and forming a bridge with the cue elevated so much isn't easy.

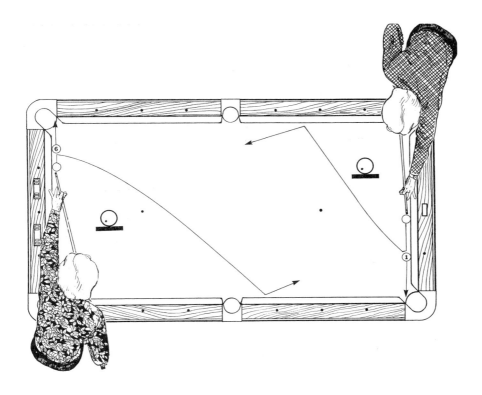

113 Frozen rail draw

With both balls frozen on the end rail, it is possible to pocket the object ball and get the cueball to the other end of the table with either follow (see previous section) or draw, provided the balls aren't too far from the pocket.

At the left, the 6-ball is only half a diamond from the pocket, which means it can be struck at a slight angle and still go in. The cueball is only a few inches farther away. With low left English, which keeps the cue from interfering with the cueball on the follow-through, the cueball will follow a path similar to the one shown. The cue is angled into the rail to ensure an off-center hit on the 6-ball. Exhibition players with powerful strokes can extend the indicated path and make the cueball hit two more rails and come to rest back at the left end of the table. I'm not one of those players.

At the right, the distances are increased and the margin of error reduced. Now the line of aim is only slightly into the rail. The hit on the 1-ball is fuller and so the cueball comes back at a sharper angle.

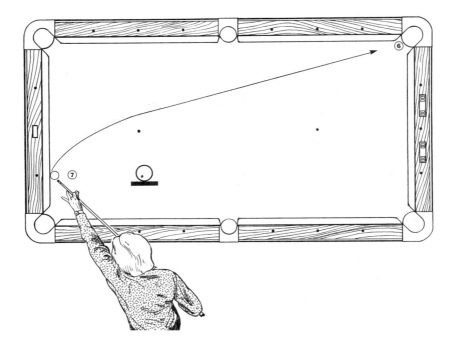

114 Rail draw

Here's an example of how to use the backspin curve off a rail to escape a hook. The most difficult position is when the cueball is frozen to the first rail, which makes it harder to deliver a foul-free stroke than it would with a gap of a few inches. (Other balls are omitted.) In the diagram, the technique is used to pocket a jawed ball, but in real life you would most likely be trying to make contact with a ball, not pocket it. The left English is to help avoid a foul.

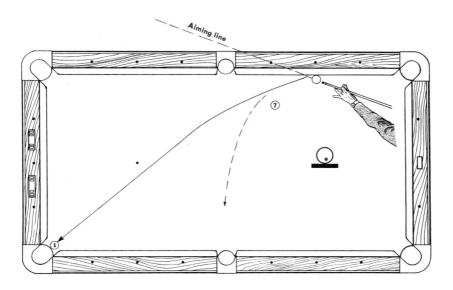

115 Rail-draw practice shot

To get the hang of the rail draw, place the cueball at the second diamond and aim at the third diamond. Use slight right English to avoid fouling. See if you can make the cueball curve enough to pocket the 1-ball. Twenty years ago I saw pro player Cicero Murphy make this shot in a game.

The dashed line indicates what is possible with draw if the cue is elevated 40 or 50 degrees. Almost anything is possible with massé.

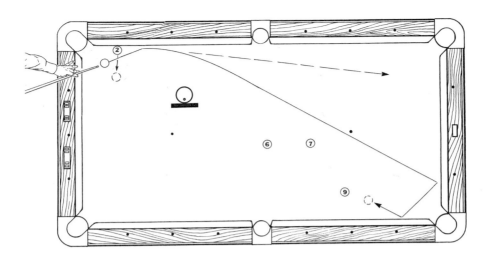

116 Thin-hit rail draw

The rail-draw curved technique also works off a ball. From the angle of approach shown, the secret is to just barely hit the 2-ball, which moves only a few inches. With a centerball hit on the cueball, it will travel along the dashed line, but with backspin and a soft hit it can be made to curve and come to rest behind blocker balls. Don't try this if you aren't confident of the feather-thin hit or if the cueball is more than a foot or two away from the object ball; with too much distance, a soft hit will allow the backspin to wear off.

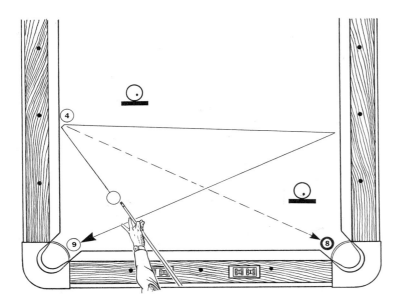

117 Rail-first cross table

These two patterns are borrowed from the three-cushion repertoire. The 4-ball is frozen. By hitting the rail before the 4-ball, the cueball can be made to cross the table and bank into the 9-ball or, with a fuller hit on the 4-ball and more draw, come straight back to the 8-ball. The pattern is more often used to play safe than to make a ball, but it's fun to dream about ending a game in spectacular fashion.

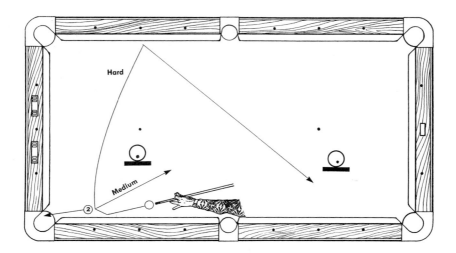

118 Rail-first up table

When the cueball and object ball are in a position as favorable as this, rail-first draw can be used to gain position. With a rather full hit on the 2-ball and a medium stroke, the cueball can be drawn toward the middle of the table. A thinner hit, a harder stroke, and a touch of right English will send the cueball on a curving path across the table and then to the right end.

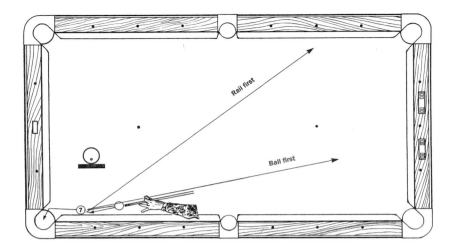

119 Rail first to frozen ball

When the object ball is this close to the pocket, even though it's frozen to the cushion, rail first is an option because the object ball will go in even if it doesn't stay on the rail. Note the very different cueball paths that result depending on whether draw is used to hit the ball first or the rail first. The rail-first pattern can save the day when other paths are blocked. For more, see Section 10 on rail-first shots.

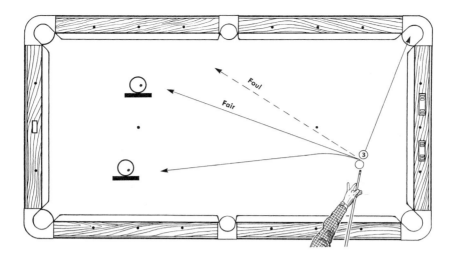

120 Small-gap draw

It's possible to draw the cueball even when the gap is very small, but you must use inside English to avoid hitting the cueball twice. Here's one place where it helps to have a crooked stroke: If you routinely swerve the cue in the direction of the English, you'll be less likely to get the double-hit foul, but more likely to miscue.

In the diagram, a foul has been committed if the cueball takes a path forward of the tangent line. Stun (no follow or draw) follows the tangent line and is legal. With a lower hit, the cueball path will curve.

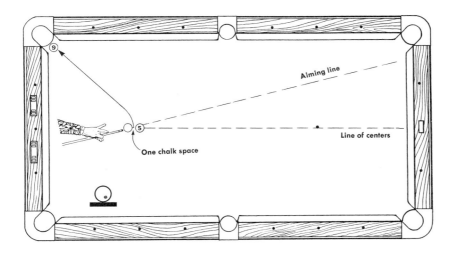

121 Extreme small-gap draw

This is close to the limit of what is possible with small-gap draw. The line of centers runs straight down the middle of the table and the 5-ball is on the foot spot. The gap is the width of a chalk cube. If you can consistently draw back and make the 9-ball, you could give me lessons.

The big strokers can squeeze even more out of this pattern, drawing the cueball back more sharply and sending it two rails all the way to the lower-right corner pocket. Three-cushion trick-shot artists can do it, too, even though a billiard table is bigger. For that action, you must aim for a fuller hit on the 5-ball and ignore the increased chance of hitting it twice. A whippy, or spindly, shaft helps because it will flex to the right at impact and thus be less likely to interfere with the cueball.

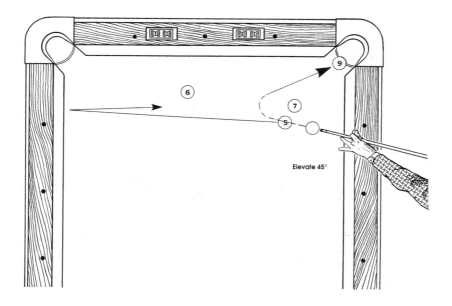

Elevate 45°

122 Jump draw

The only way to make the cueball advance beyond an object ball before drawing back is to shoot a jump shot. The famous over-and-under trick shot is based on this principle (see *Byrne's Treasury of Trick Shots* [1982], page 9).

Diagrammed here is a hypothetical position from a game of nine-ball. There are safeties to consider, but if you don't mind taking a chance, the balls are well placed for a jump draw. Elevate the cue about 35 to 45 degrees, hit the cueball well below center, and shoot fairly hard. The cueball will bounce once or twice before the draw grabs. This technique isn't for everybody.

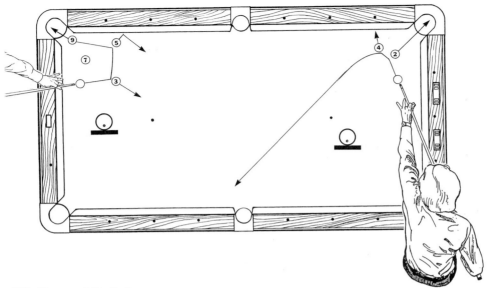

123 Second-ball draw

At the right is another example of cutting a ball thin and drawing off the second ball. At the left is one of my favorite shots; I sometimes set it up and shoot it just for fun. The cueball describes a square as it goes from one ball to another. How would you like to make this shot in a tournament game? Keep your eyes open, and maybe Fortune will smile on you.

In a trick-shot show, use a ball tray as interference instead of the 7-ball.

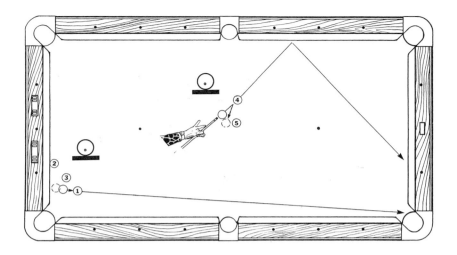

124 Deadball draw

The opposite of lively draw—achieved by hitting the cueball very low with speed appropriate to the distance to the object ball—is deadball draw. The cueball comes back slowly and stops short of the maximum distance. You need to hit the cueball just a little below center or reduce the speed of the cueball, or both. Opportunities to use deadball draw come up all the time in position play, and an ability to execute it well is a powerful weapon. To practice, shoot a series of stop shots of varying distances, then shoot them again and try to make the cueball back up a few inches.

In the diagram are two safety plays. Would you think of playing safe in the center of the table by drawing off the 4-ball to place the cueball behind the 5-ball? It's a shot worth practicing. At the lower left, you must drive the 1-ball the length of the table and draw the cueball back a short distance for a shot at the 2-ball. Precise control is difficult when the distance between the cueball and the object ball is a foot or more.

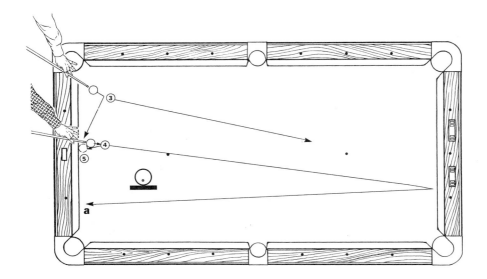

125 Deadball safeties

Two more deadball-draw safeties are illustrated here. At the top, the 3-ball is driven to the right end of the table and back to a spot near *a* at the left end. The cueball moves slowly to the rail and stops snuggled up to the 5 as shown by the dashed ball. Another challenge is to drive the 4-ball eighteen feet and draw the cueball five inches as shown at the left center of the diagram. Set the two shots up and see how many times you can hide the cueball behind the 5-ball in ten tries.

Himmel! ein Loch und gewiß das Erste. Zehn Gulden!

Sapperlot, springt der aus und gerade in den Spiegel!

The first law of billiards: If something can go wrong, it will.

Courtesy Heinrich Weingartner, Weingartner Museum of Billiards

"Stun" is a term I borrowed years ago from the English game of snooker to describe shots in which the cueball hits an object ball with no (or very little) topspin or backspin. In others words, the cueball is sliding rather than rolling at the moment of impact. A sliding cueball that hits an object ball squarely stops dead in its tracks: the so-called stop shot. It pays to master it at all distances.

If a sliding cueball hits an object ball at an angle, it caroms off along the tangent line (the right-angle line). It takes experience, judgment, and touch to make the cueball roll to a stop at any given point on the tangent line.

A cueball struck in the exact center (on the equator) starts out sliding and gradually takes on natural roll. If the cueball is only a foot or two from the object ball, hitting the cueball in the center with a firm stroke will cause it to stop on impact with the object ball, but for greater distances, draw must be used, unless you shoot extremely hard. At the length of the table, use maximum backspin and choose a speed that allows the backspin to wear off just as the cueball hits the object ball and before it has picked up natural roll. Doing that consistently at distances of five feet or more takes considerable skill.

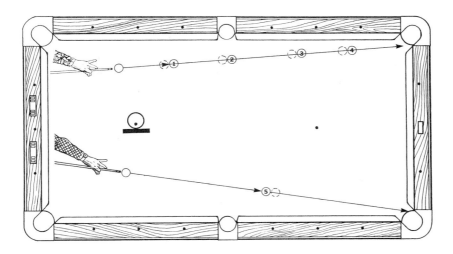

126 Stun practice

At the top are straight-in shots at various distances. To stop the cueball at impact with no sideways drift requires both slide and a dead-center hit, not easy at a distance of six feet. Many a position play is ruined when a lack of precision on the object-ball hit causes the cueball to drift right or left along the tangent line.

In the diagram, a centerball hit will suffice for the 1-ball if firm speed is used. To stop the cueball and make the 4-ball requires a low hit on the cueball.

At the bottom, the goal is to make the 5-ball and let the cueball follow just a few inches. To do that, the cueball must have stopped sliding and picked up just a little natural roll. Pro snooker players are uncanny at making the cueball roll any desired distance after the impact, a shot they call "stun run-through."

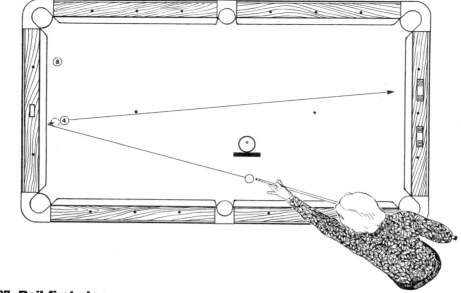

127 Rail-first stop

This common safety play is, in fact, a stop shot. Unless the balls and the cloth are very slippery, shooting into a rail at an angle this close to perpendicular causes the cueball to rebound with no topspin. If you can manage a full hit on the 4-ball, the cueball will stay in place.

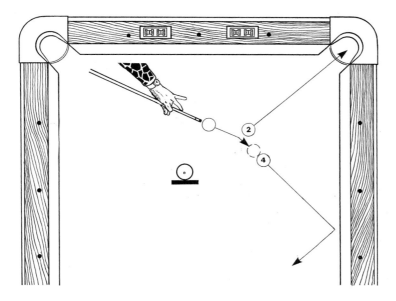

128 Second-ball stop

To make the 2-ball, you must hit it thin and use a lot of speed to guarantee that it reaches the pocket. If you want to stay at the same end of the table and you can manage a full hit on the 4-ball, hit the cueball in the center. Because of the speed required to cut the 2-ball in, the cueball will be sliding when it hits the 4-ball.

As we have already seen, you can draw back from the 4 or follow through it by using backspin or topspin.

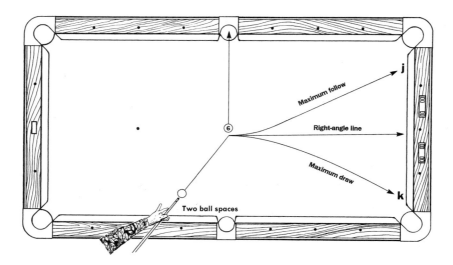

129 **More stun practice**

From this position, practice sending the cueball exactly along the right-angle line to the center of the end rail. Reaching point *j* requires maximum follow and point *k* maximum draw.

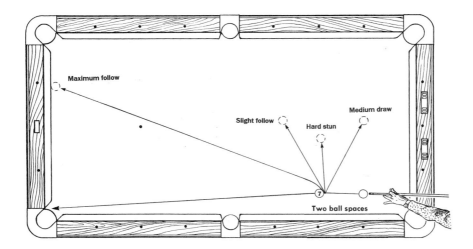

130 Still more practice

Both the cueball and the 7-ball are two ball widths from the rail. It is possible to make the cueball follow any of the four paths. The slight follow path is achieved by hitting the cueball just a little above center; medium draw requires a below-center hit, but something less than you would use for maximum backspin. It takes a lot of practice to master the in between topspins and backspins. Most players don't even realize they should be practicing them.

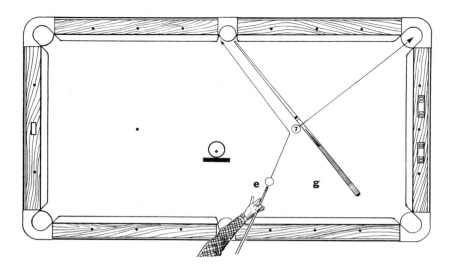

131 **The right-angle principle**

Here's a way to improve your stun stroke. Lay your cue on the table so that it points directly at the edge of the side pocket. It doesn't have to be exactly as shown in the diagram. Now put the 7-ball against the cue so that a line from it to the corner is perpendicular to the cue. Remove the cue. With the cueball anywhere around point *e,* a perfect stop shot will send the 7-ball into the corner and the cueball into the side.

Put the cueball at or near point *g* and shoot the 7-ball into the side. Perfect stop action will result in a scratch in the corner.

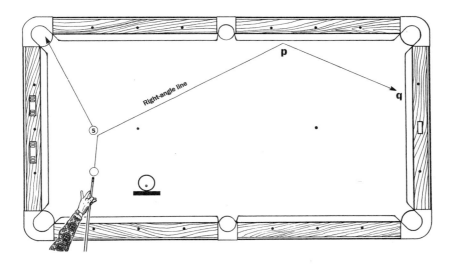

132 Tangent-line practice

To play good position, you must be able to stop the cueball at any desired point on the right-angle line. From the given position, adjust the speed to make the cueball roll to a stop at either *p* or *q*. You are doing it right if the cueball travels in a straight line from the 5-ball. A deviation from the right-angle line means there was follow or draw on the cueball.

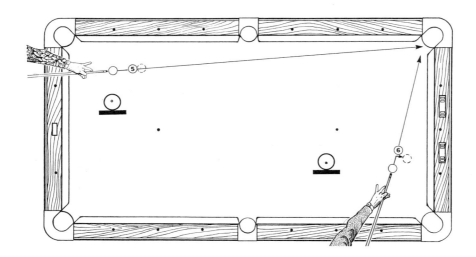

133 Useful applications

At the top, the 5-ball is straight in. Let's say you want to make the 5-ball and stop the cueball a few inches forward as indicated by the dashed ball. To give the cueball just a little forward roll at impact, hit it just slightly above center.

If you want to make the cueball roll forward a foot, you have two choices. One is to use a very soft stroke with topspin. If the speed is such that the 5-ball barely reaches the pocket, the cueball will stop after rolling forward a foot or so. The second choice is to use just a little topspin and a firmer stroke. A top professional player, by shooting firmly and varying only the amount of topspin, can cause the cueball to roll to a stop anywhere along the line with a margin of error of six inches or so.

At the right is what I call the popover shot. It's straight in, but for positional reasons you want to make the cueball pop over to the right a few inches. To do it, hit the cueball in the center—it's so close to the 6-ball it won't have time to pick up any follow—and cheat the pocket to the left. This shot comes up all the time in straight pool, especially line-up straight pool. In that game you have to be able to shoot firmly and move the cueball small distances with precision.

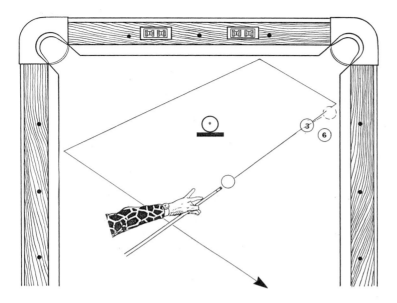

134 Stun run-through for safety

Maybe I haven't convinced you that stun run-through is better than slow rolling. Diagrammed is a safety shot that can be executed only with stun run-through. The idea is to leave the cueball behind the 6-ball while banking the 3-ball three rails. Using slow speed won't send the 3-ball far enough. The correct method is to give the 3 plenty of speed while hitting the cueball just a little above center. If the cueball hasn't picked up full natural roll, it will snuggle in behind the 6-ball for a vicious safety.

This is often a game-winning maneuver because your opponent is apt to sell out on his turn if he can't see the 3-ball.

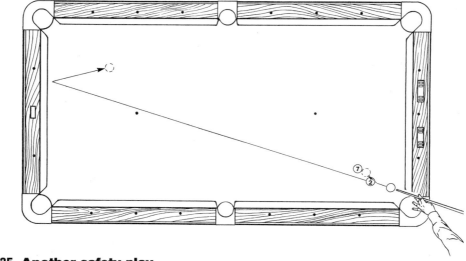

135 Another safety play

The goal is to snooker your opponent behind the 7-ball. (Other balls are omitted.) You have to shoot hard enough to send the 2-ball to the left end rail; otherwise it's a foul. But with full topspin on the cueball, it will bump into the 7-ball with too much speed. With just a hair of topspin, though, the cueball will come to rest nicely behind the 7 as shown by the dashed ball.

NOTE: When playing safe, don't leave the ball your opponent must hit close to a rail because that presents a bigger target for a kick.

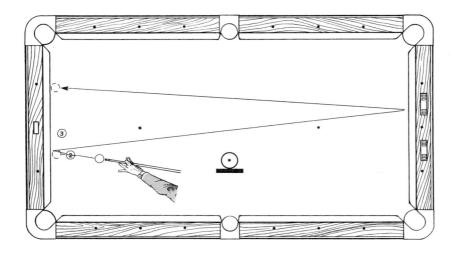

136 An eighteen-foot safety

Hardly anybody would think of playing the safety diagrammed here, but it isn't difficult if you are used to the stun run-through shot. (Other balls omitted.) Hitting the cueball just a hair above center will make it move forward only a few inches while the 2-ball travels twice the length of the table. It's easier than it looks because the position of the 3-ball provides a sizeable margin of error. There's something satisfying about this shot. I try it every month or so while practicing just to see if I can make it on the first attempt. If it ever comes up in a game, I'll jump on it.

RAIL FIRST 10

What people watched, before
television ruined everything.
Courtesy Heinrich Weingartner,
Weingartner Museum of Billiards

When an object ball is close to the rail as well as close to a pocket, going rail first with the cueball is always an option. The speed and direction of the cueball are much different if you hit the rail before the ball, as the following examples show. In many situations, it's practical to hit the rail first even if the object ball is frozen to the rail, a fact that is seldom exploited under game conditions even though the shot is not particularly difficult.

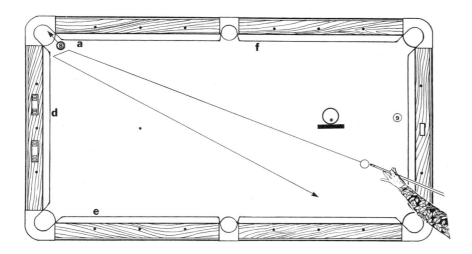

137 Rail-first option

Your opponent got position on the 9-ball but jawed the 8-ball. Your job is to make the 8-ball and get down table for the 9. This is one of the most treacherous shots in pool. Hit the 8-ball a little too full and the cueball loses its speed; too thin and it has too much speed. Here it is especially tricky because if you hit the left side of the 8 too thin, it may hit the point of the pocket and not go in. A subtle method of handling a shot like this is shown in the diagram. Use a low hit and try to slide the cueball into the left side of the 8-ball; when the cueball rebounds from the end rail, there will be no topspin to kill the speed and the cueball will travel down the table as shown. Right English with slide action brings the cueball down the rail to *f*.

Another option is to hit the rail first at point *a*, sending the cueball to *d*, *e*, and *f* and down to the right end rail. That's a good choice if you have enough judgment to avoid scratching in the side off the third rail.

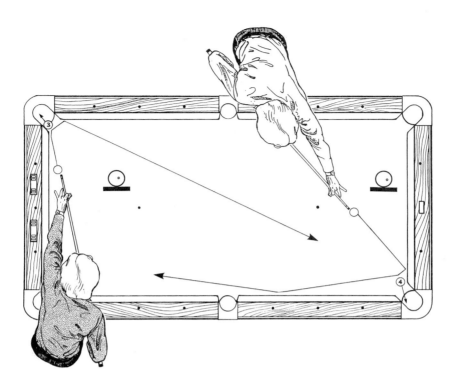

138 Simple rail firsts

In both of these shots, it's hard to hit the jawed ball first and get the cueball to the other end of the table for position. At the left, the cueball might hit the point of the pocket if you hit the 3-ball first. At the right, the shot is straight in. One option is to cut the 4-ball slightly, use high right with a hard stroke, and try to send the cueball off two rails with strong follow action.

Better is the rail-first shot, which can be hit with surprisingly little speed.

Backspin instead of running English on both shots will keep the cueball closer to the long rails as it goes down table.

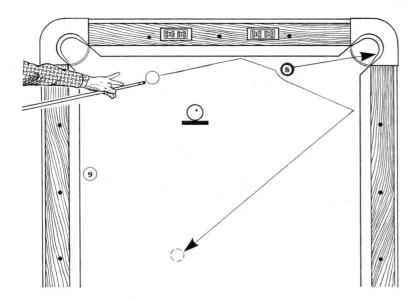

139 Rail-first follow

The shot on the 8-ball is straight in, which makes it tough to get position on the 9-ball along the left long rail. The 8-ball is far enough away from the pocket that any attempt to cheat the pocket is hazardous. The rail-first follow shot as diagrammed is an attractive option. The difficulty increases with the distance from the pocket and the distance from the object ball to the rail.

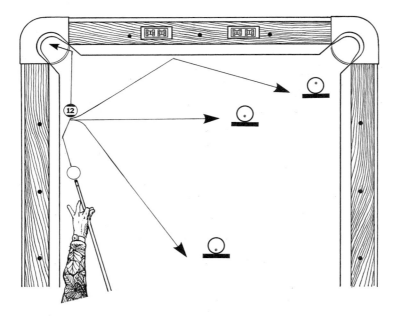

140 Rail-first flexibility

When the position is this easy, a knowledgeable player can make the 12-ball and leave the cueball anywhere on the table. Beginners would think only of the straight-in shot. The three rail-first paths in the diagram result from follow, stun, and draw.

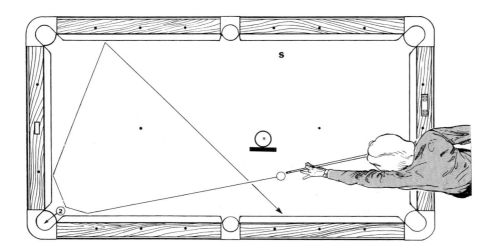

141 Standard four-rail pattern

When the object ball and cueball are placed as favorably as this, there is a large margin of error on making the shot and great freedom in positioning the cueball off two, three, four, and five rails. You have to be familiar enough with the angles that you can miss the scratch in the side off three rails. The scratch is more likely if the cueball starts at point *s* because from there it's hard to hit the cueball thin enough off the first rail.

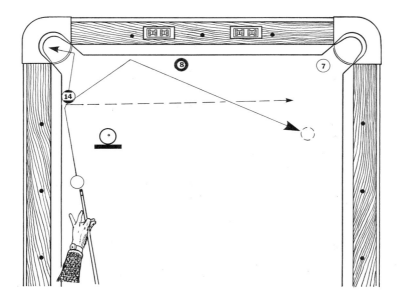

142 Frozen rail-first

If you are not familiar with frozen rail-first shots, you are about to learn something that is worth the price of the book. A ball frozen to a rail can be made in a
corner pocket either by hitting the ball and the rail at the same time, provided
you use just the right amount of outside English (without which, throw will
send the object ball into the rail and out again), or by hitting the rail before the
ball. Whether or not the cueball hits the rail first can't be seen by the naked eye
at the moment of impact, but the difference in the path of the cueball afterward
is dramatic.

Diagrammed is a position from a game of eight-ball. How can you make
the 14-ball and get position on the 8-ball, given that the right corner pocket is
blocked? The answer is to hit the rail first. With high right and medium speed,
the cueball will follow the solid line while spinning like a top. With stop-shot
action, a stronger speed, and a rail-first hit, the cueball will travel along the
dashed line for position on the 8.

Note that hitting the 14-ball first with high right won't get the job done.
With enough follow and right spin, it might be possible to get the cueball to a
spot near the right side pocket (off the diagram), but the cut on the 8-ball would
be tough to make from there.

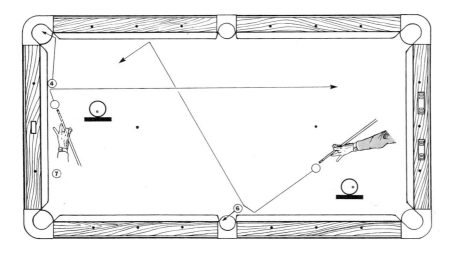

143 Two little-known patterns

At the right, the player is faced with a shot on the 6-ball straight into the side. Is it possible to make the 6-ball and get a good shot at the 7-ball? Yes, by hitting the side rail first with running English and low speed. This would be overlooked by many players.

At the left, it seems that the 4-ball is too straight in to make and still get the cueball to the right end of the table. It is easy if you hit the rail first. Shown is the result if you slide the cueball into the 4. Follow and draw can also be used if balls are blocking the diagrammed path.

Please note that on rail-first shots of this type, the object ball may stay on the rail all the way into the pocket because the cueball sinks into the rubber before hitting the ball. (For a full discussion of this point, see *Byrne's Advanced Technique in Pool and Billiards* [1990], pages 27–30.) But even if the object ball leaves the rail, there is a good margin of error when it is this close to the pocket.

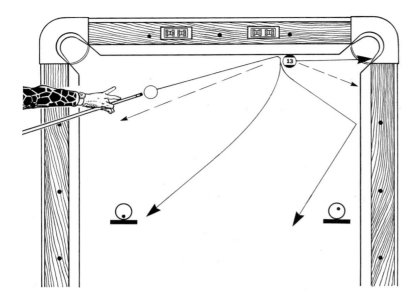

144 Draw and follow

You have a lot of freedom on a shot like this, even though it may not seem so at first glance. The dashed lines indicate what happens to the cueball when you use follow and draw and hit the 13-ball first. The curved solid lines show the results when you use follow and draw and hit the rail before the ball. With this knowledge you can make some beautiful position plays.

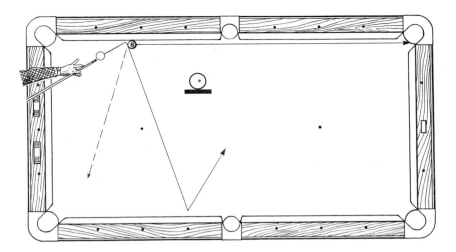

145 **The basic principle**

Here is the secret of the frozen-ball shot reduced to a minimum. How often can you run the 8-ball down the rail past the side pocket and into the corner? Two or three times out of ten tries would be commendable for the uneducated. Now that you know the secret of hitting the rail slightly first, you should be able to make it seven or eight times out of ten. (I just tried it and made nine out of ten, and I'm not a great shotmaker.) The cueball will carom off the 8-ball roughly as indicated by the solid line. Why this works is explained on page 24 of *Byrne's Advanced Technique in Pool and Billiards* (1990).

The shot is also makeable by hitting the 8-ball and the rail at the same time using outside (left, in this case) English to eliminate the throw effect. This approach brings the cueball off the rail along the dashed line. Throw is eliminated by outside English because the cueball rolls off the object ball instead of rubbing against it during the millisecond of contact.

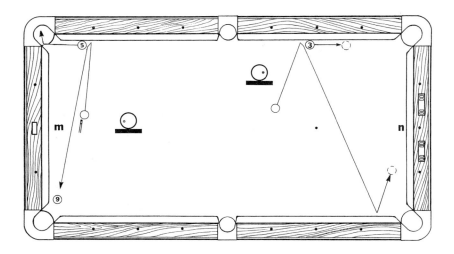

146 The impossible cut

At the upper left, there seems to be no way to cut the 5-ball into the corner pocket because the necessary contact point can't be "seen" by the cueball. The shot can be made by shooting to barely miss the 5-ball with heavy left English on the cueball. As the cueball comes off the rail, it touches the 5-ball just enough to send it down the rail and into the pocket. A scratch is always a possibility with this pattern, but if the lower-left corner pocket is blocked by a ball—in this case the 9—the technique can be used to make it. The shot really is impossible if you hit the 5-ball first.

You think you are a great player? Freeze an object ball at point *n* and put the cueball at point *m,* six inches off the rail. Using the idea of hitting the rail just before the object ball, cut the ball at *n* into either corner pocket. It can be done, but you have to be good.

At the upper right is a rail-first safety shot to consider if the corner pocket is blocked.

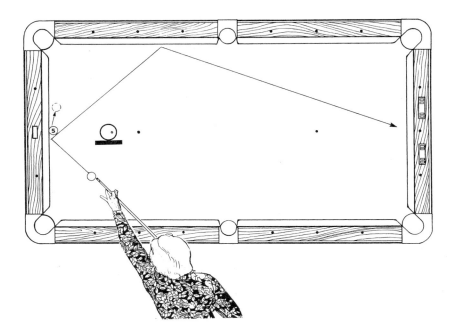

147 Rail-first safety

Try this safety shot with the balls placed exactly as shown. It takes practice to hit the 5-ball thin enough to keep it from moving more than a few inches. Shoot softly with maximum sidespin. On your first attempt you are likely to use too much speed and hit too much of the 5-ball.

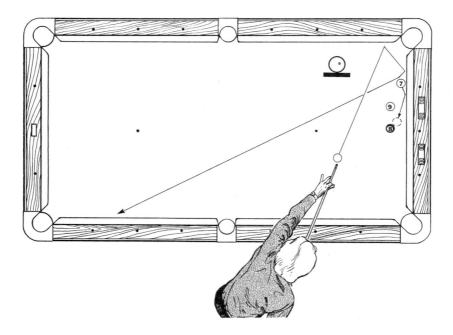

148 Two rails first—I

It often isn't enough just to hit the correct ball to escape from a safety; you have to hit it thick or thin and on the proper side. One reason the great Efren Reyes is so hard to beat is that he is an excellent three-cushion player and can estimate multiple-rail kicks with uncanny accuracy. Diagrammed is a two-rail kick shot. If the cueball hits the 7-ball thin, the result is a safety as shown. Hit the 7-ball too full and you have sold out.

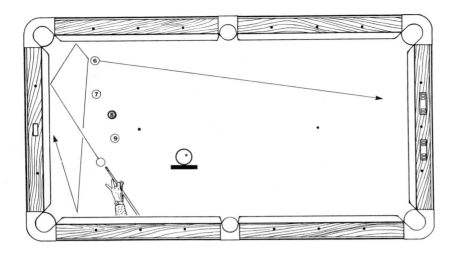

149 Two rails first—II

This two-rail kick is not easy, because it depends on moving both the object ball and the cueball a considerable distance. The key is to hit the correct side of the first ball. It is much easier to calculate a safety shot if you only have to concern yourself with the roll of one ball.

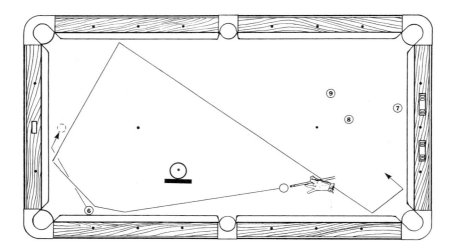

150 Another rail-first safety

The game is nine-ball. It is extremely difficult to make the 6-ball and get shape on the 7-ball at the other end of the table. Something to consider in the given position is a rail-first safety. A thin hit on the 6-ball will move it toward the center of the left end rail and send the cueball three or four rails to the right end rail.

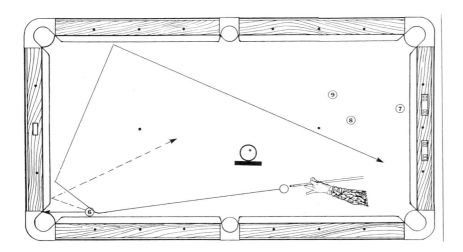

151 A second option

This is the same position as shown in the previous diagram. Let's say you don't like the rail-first safety and decide to make the 6-ball instead. If you make the 6 and fail to get position, you can play safe off the 7-ball. Hitting the ball first with follow will send the cueball along the dashed line or close to it, which isn't very promising. Hitting the rail slightly before the 6-ball is the winning ticket. The 6-ball goes in and the cueball takes the solid-line path around the table. The disadvantage is that it takes considerable precision to hit the rail first and still make the 6 from such a distance. Still, it's the best choice, in my opinion.

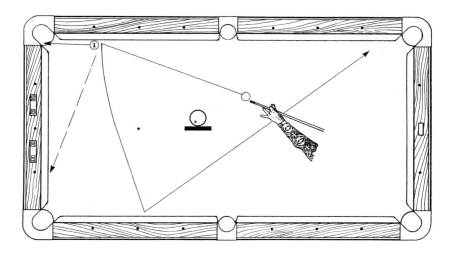

152 Rail-first stroke shot

With draw and left sidespin, it is possible to hit the rail first, make the 1-ball, and bring the cueball back to the right end of the table. You need a very good draw stroke to execute this shot. The big strokers love it.

With the same spin on the cueball, a ball-first hit will send the cueball in the direction of the dashed line.

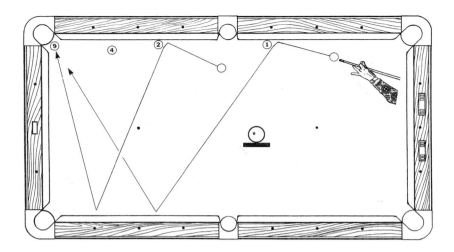

153 Rail first to score

The 9-ball is hanging on the lip. If you decide to try to make it off the 1-ball, the best bet is hit the rail first with left sidespin. The same is true from the other cue-ball if the 2-ball is the lowest ball on the table. Try these patterns and I think you'll agree that they are better choices than anything involving ball-first hits. With more balls on the table, the same patterns might be good for safety plays.

Herr Kugelich fpielt Billard.

Over time, some people grow to resemble their hobbies.

Billard Welt magazine, Berlin, 1913

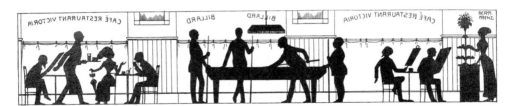

The scene in Café Restaurant Victoria

Billard Welt magazine, Berlin, 1913

onventional wisdom holds that the harder you shoot a bank shot, the "shorter" it goes, yet many teachers and instructional books state that the angle of a ball going into a rail is the same as the angle coming out. You can't have it both ways. In fact, the angle of incidence is seldom exactly equal to the angle of reflection (as physicists would put it).

When a naturally rolling ball rebounds from a cushion, the topspin bends its path forward and it banks "long." Any sidespin the ball has when it hits the cushion also, of course, affects the rebound angle.

As for the effect of speed, it is more helpful to consider roll and slide rather than speed. Faced with a bank shot, you must take account of the English, if any, the cueball will impart to the object ball due to sidespin or the angle of approach, *but you must also estimate the amount of roll or slide the ball will have when it hits the rail.* A ball that slides into a rail (no topspin or backspin) rebounds at close to the same angle regardless of speed. The rebound angle of a rolling ball is also largely immune to changes in speed.

The significant influence of slide and roll in banking was first mentioned in the literature in my *Billiards Digest* magazine article, February 1987, pages 20–21, and in *Byrne's Advanced Technique in Pool and Billiards* (1990), pages 42–44.

A lot of misleading advice has been published about bank shots and how to make them. By the end of this section you'll have a better understanding of why the shot is so often missed and how you can increase your success rate.

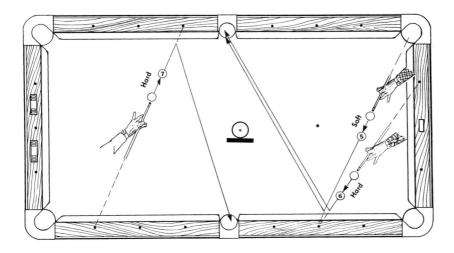

154 Long and short

The 5-ball bank is set up so that the angles from the first-rail contact point to the side pocket and the corner pocket are the same. Note how the axis of the cue passes over the middle of the corner pocket and how the 5-ball is aimed at the second diamond. Shoot softly and the shot will bank into the side: the angle that the 5-ball goes into the rail is the same as the angle coming out. (Well, not quite, because the ball is aimed at the diamond, not at the point on the nose of the cushion opposite the diamond.)

Now try the 6-ball bank. The axis of the cue passes over the first diamond on the end rail. The 6-ball is only six inches or so from the side rail. Shoot *hard* and the bank works.

At the left, the line of aim runs from the first diamond on the long rail to the first diamond to the left of the side pocket. Shoot hard and the bank goes; shoot softly and the 7-ball will land a foot beyond the side pocket.

The differing bank angles result from slide and roll.

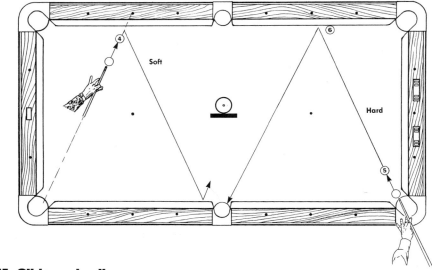

155 Slide and roll

The two banks diagrammed here have the same line of aim: from the corner to the second diamond. The only difference is that in one case the object ball is far from the rail and in the other it is very close to the rail. It may surprise you to find out that if you hit the 4-ball softly it will come in short, while if you hit the 5-ball as hard as you can it will make...or come close to making. This is the complete opposite of what most players think—that high speed makes banks come short.

What's going on? The 4-ball is so close to the rail that even when struck softly it will slide into the cushion because it doesn't have enough time or space to begin rolling. In fact, no matter how much speed you use, it will bank to the same point. At the right, the 5-ball will bank long at all speeds because even if you hit it as hard as you can, it will be rolling by the time it gets to the rail and will take a longer angle because of the slight bend the topspin imparts to the rebound path.

The two shots prove that speed isn't the controlling factor in bank shots. What counts are slide and roll. If you want to try the shots yourself, place a 6-ball as shown to make sure you don't drive the 5-ball to the right of the diamond.

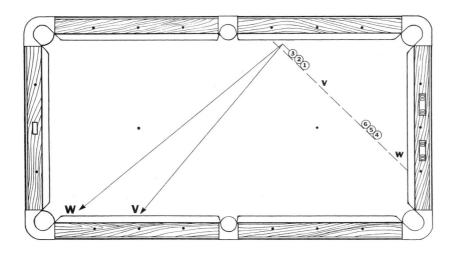

156 The three-balls test

Irrefutable proof of how slide and roll control banking angles is provided by two three-ball combinations. Wedge your cue into the long and short rails as indicated by the dashed line. Use the side of the cue to align two three-ball combinations. Locate the 1-2-3 so that the 3-ball is less than a ball space from the cushion. Position the 4-5-6 three or four feet farther back. (The combinations remove throw and imperfect hits as factors.) Remove your cue. Place the cueball at point *v* and strike the 1-ball just hard enough so the 3-ball reaches the second rail at point *V.* Clear the 1-2-3 from the table and place the cueball at *w.* Hit the 4-ball as hard as you want and you will find that the 6-ball banks to *W.* The reason the 6-ball banks long is that it will be rolling when it reaches the first rail no matter how hard you hit the 4-ball. In both cases, the balls rebound at close to the same angles at all speeds.

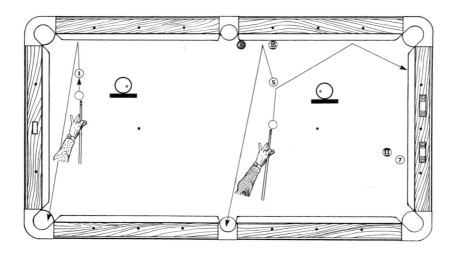

157 Transfer of spin—I

Approximately 2 percent of a cueball's sidespin is transferred to an object ball on a full hit—more if the balls are dirty or old. At the left, the two balls are the same distance from the left end rail. Hit the 1-ball full in the face with heavy right English and it can be made to bank in the corner, thanks to English-induced throw and transfer of spin. If the cueball does not drift to the right, you'll know you didn't cut the 1-ball to the left. The shot is easier than the similar one shown in Section 5, diagram 68, because not as much throw is required.

At the right, the goal is to bank the 5-ball and get position on the 7-ball. Required is a stroke strong enough to send the 5-ball sliding into the rail along with left English on the cueball to give the 5-ball a touch of right. The left spin on the cueball kills its speed off the two rails it contacts.

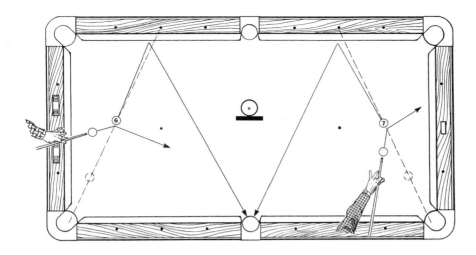

158 Transfer of spin—II

Both balls are on a dashed line running from the corner to the second diamond. If they were struck full by the cueball on the same line (dashed balls), they would bank in the side. At the left, cutting the 6-ball gives it a little right English because of the friction at the moment of contact. The angle of approach to the rail, therefore, must be altered.

At the right, the collision between the balls gives the 7-ball a little right English, which means that it must be hit slightly thinner than the geometry suggests to compensate for the sidespin.

To avoid what can be called cut-induced throw, use outside English so that at the moment of contact, the cueball rolls off the object ball instead of rubbing against it. How much outside English? That depends on the angle of the cut.

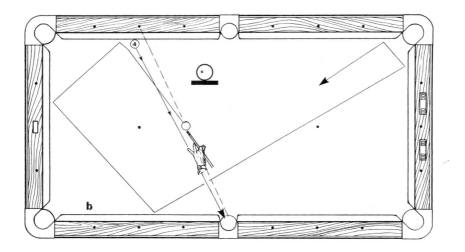

159 Maximum angle

On my table, this is the absolute limit for a backward bank. Note the exact position of the balls. Put the balls in place on a table and study the scene for a moment to familiarize yourself with the limits of the possible. With a thin hit and a hard stroke, the 4-ball just barely reaches the side pocket while the cueball circumnavigates the table to end at point *b* on the sixth rail.

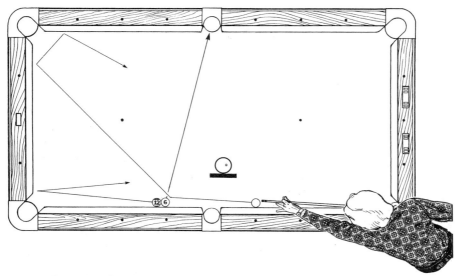

160 Ball-induced spin

It's counterintuitive, but the 6-ball can be banked from this unpromising position. Use right English and hit about a third of the 6-ball. It will pick up just enough sidespin as it rubs against the 12-ball to send it across the table on an unexpected path. The idea is more practical than it seems. Move all three balls a foot away from the rail and it still works.

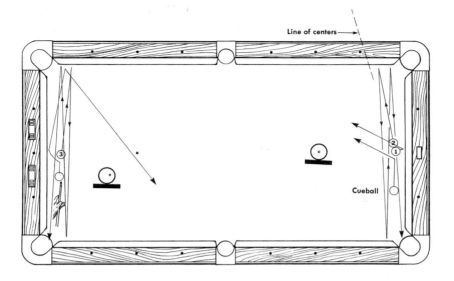

Line of centers

Cueball

161 Triple banks

At the left, the 3-ball and the cueball are both a ball width from the rail. Nevertheless, the 3-ball can be triple-banked into the lower-left-hand corner, which might be desirable if the upper-left corner pocket is blocked. Use a hard stroke, cut the 3 slightly to the right, and use plenty of right English. It's easier to miss an immediate kiss if you place the 3-ball a half inch farther from the rail than the cueball.

The triple bank at the right is even more surprising. Note the line of centers of the combination. By shooting the cueball into the left side of the 1-ball, the 2-ball is not only thrown to the right, it is given a little right sidespin.

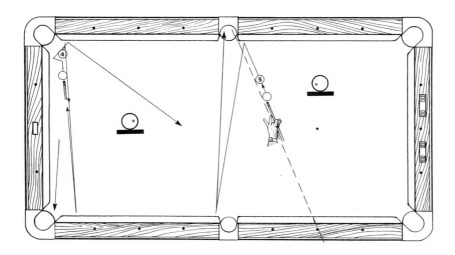

162 Double and triple

There doesn't seem to be any way to make the 4-ball in the lower-left corner, but it can be triple-banked. Use right sidespin and cut the 4-ball just enough to the right to avoid the kiss.

At the right, the 5-ball can be banked to a point beyond the lower side pocket and into the upper side pocket. Align the balls by laying your cue on the table on the dashed line. Use a hard stroke and maximum left English.

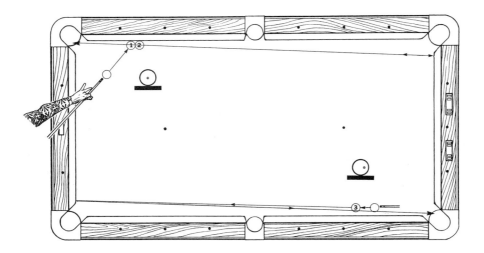

163 **The long way**

Freeze the 1-ball and the 2-ball as shown. Hit the 1-ball from the given cueball position and watch what happens. The 2-ball is thrown into the rail and out again, but sometimes picks up enough sidespin to hit the right end rail and rebound into the upper-left corner pocket. Don't bet on it.

At the bottom, the percentage is a little higher. Both balls are one ball width from the cushion, which seems to rule out a bank shot. But the 3-ball can be banked with the help of sidespin transferred from the cueball.

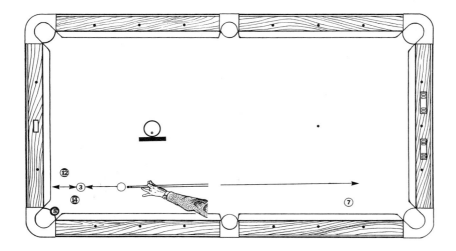

164 Kick-back strategy

The game is eight-ball and you have the solids. The 8-ball is blocking the corner pocket. It wouldn't help to make the 7-ball, and while there are various ways to play safe off the right side of the 3-ball, they don't improve your chances, and they give your opponent a chance to play safe in return. An ingenious play is to hit the 3-ball squarely with low backspin so that it banks off the end rail and back into cueball. With the right speed, the cueball will end up near the 7-ball, and the 3-ball will be near the side pocket. You are now a big favorite to win because the 3-ball is away from the blocked pocket and it's hard for your opponent to lay down a decent safety.

The position shown is contrived, but the idea of banking a ball back into the cueball is occasionally useful in safety play.

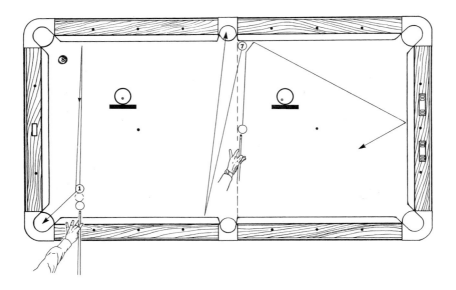

165 A stop carom and a double bank

At the left is a clever one-pocket shot, or, as set up in the diagram, a shot to try in a game of eight-ball when both a one-rail bank and a straight-in shot are blocked. Shoot the 1-ball straight across the table, stop the cueball dead, and pray that the 1-ball comes back and kisses off the cueball into the pocket.

In the center, the cueball and the object ball are located as indicated by the dashed line. Willie Jopling says that the great Eddie Taylor could bank the 7-ball into the lower side pocket. The rest of us have to be content with a double bank.

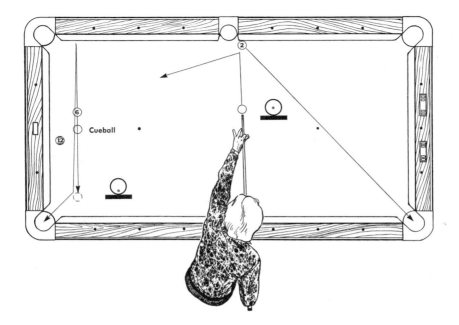

166 A moving carom and a kiss bank

Thinking about the stop carom in the previous diagram led me to invent a moving carom that is lovely when it works. The 6-ball can't be banked because of the 12-ball. Drive the 6-ball straight across the table and draw the cueball toward the lower rail. With luck, the 6-ball will come back and kiss off the moving cueball and go into the pocket. It's not quite as hard as it looks, because the margin of error on the carom is fairly large. It's demonstrated on *Byrne's Gamebreakers,* a videotape produced in 2002 by Accu-Stats.

In the center, it looks impossible to bank the 2-ball without scratching in the side. Hitting enough of the 2-ball to get a double kiss avoids the scratch. It might be worth a try in some positions.

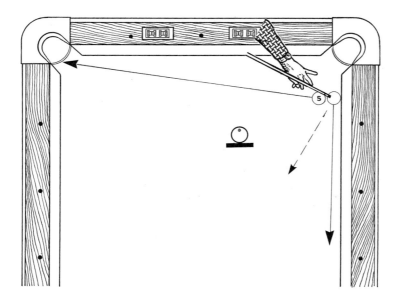

167 **Frozen kick back**

The cueball is frozen to the rail but not to the 5-ball. Shooting toward the 5-ball is an almost certain double-hit foul. Shooting into the rail and hitting the cueball very high with an elevated cue is probably not a foul, especially if the cueball travels down the rail as shown. If the cueball comes sharply off the rail (dashed line), it means you hit it twice.

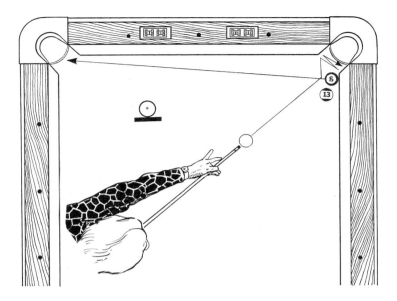

168 Pocket-point escape

Can the 8-ball be banked in this position? Yes, if you can manage to carom into the pocket point. The cueball doesn't always rattle in the jaws as shown—its exact path is unpredictable—but if you can hit the point you'll probably miss both the kiss and the scratch.

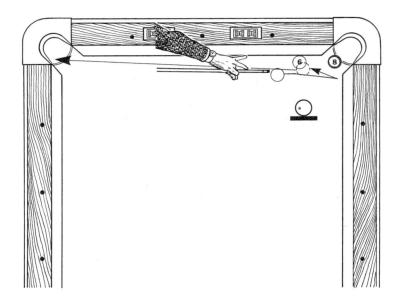

169 Time shot

A great idea from the game of one-pocket is adapted here to eight-ball. The concept involves relocating the object ball so that it can be kicked into the opposite corner pocket. Hit the 6-ball thin. Left spin on the cueball brings it off the rail and squarely into the 6. Making this shot is a one-in-ten chance, but worth a try if the rest of the table is tied up.

SIDE POCKETS

The stylish Ralph Greenleaf was the man to beat in 1932.

From the Byrne collection

B ecause of the side pocket's design and location at the middle of each long rail, certain scoring and positional moves can be made at the side pockets that aren't possible or feasible at the corners. Some are well known, some aren't.

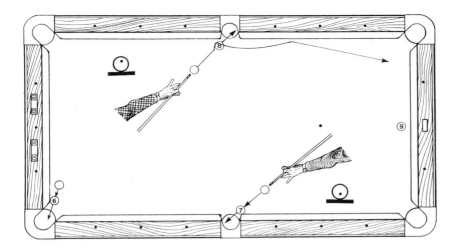

170 Scoring and position

The 8-ball at the top isn't quite straight in. The problem for the player who wants to get position on the 9-ball at the right end rail is that the 8 can't be cut to the left. The solution is to cut it slightly to the right with topspin. The cueball will follow a curving path approximately as shown. The action is fairly easy to get at close quarters, but difficult if the 8-ball is more than an inch or two from the rail.

At the bottom, the 7-ball is touching the cushion. If it is not too far away from the point, it can be driven straight into the pocket with a hard, full-in-the-face hit—the rubber simply bends out of the way.

At the lower-left corner is the same idea applied to a corner pocket—useful when any cut on the 6-ball would lose position.

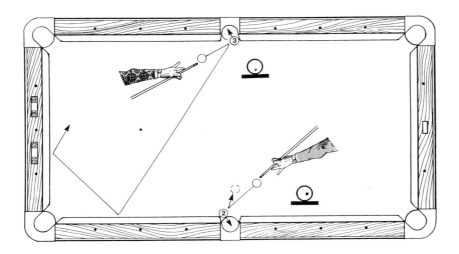

171 Two kiss-backs

At the bottom, the 2-ball is frozen, or close to frozen, to the pocket point, but from the cueball position it can't be cut in. The ball can still be made, though, with a full hit, maximum right sidespin, and soft speed. Enough sidespin is transferred to the 2-ball to force it to the left and over the edge of the slate. The cueball will kiss back as shown. Even if the 2-ball can be cut in with a thin hit, the kiss shot might be better for positional reasons.

At the top, the 3-ball is deeper into the pocket and can be cut in. The player has an option: a kiss-back with low right will send the cueball on the diagrammed path. Firm speed can be used because the shot is hard to miss.

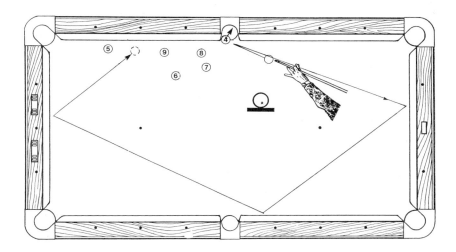

172 Around-the-table kiss-back

If the object ball is deep in the jaws, you don't need to rely on cueball spin to force it into the pocket—almost any movement will send it over the edge and in. With a setup like that you can use draw and *right* English and send the cueball off three or four rails. As a challenge to a friend, set up the diagrammed position and see if he or she can make the 4-ball and get position on the 5-ball. My thanks to Tom Rossman for this one.

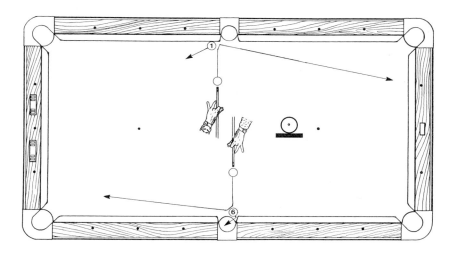

173 **Off the points**

At the top, the position of the 1-ball and the cueball allows for an unusual safety pattern. Hit the 1-ball first, then the pocket point, and the cueball will rebound to the right end of the table. This move can be considered whenever you are confident that you can get a precise enough hit to carom the cueball into the point without scratching.

At the bottom, you don't have to thin cut the 6-ball to make it. You can double-kiss it into the side. Because of the double kiss, the cueball goes to the left end of the table for position.

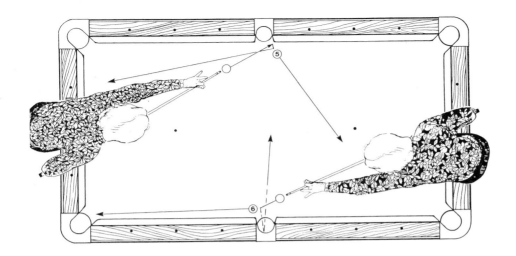

174 Avoiding scratches—I

A common problem in pool is making a ball in the corner without scratching in the side. When the balls are located as shown at the bottom of the diagram, a brilliant but risky solution is to elevate the butt of the cue and jump the cueball off the 6-ball into the back rim of the pocket so that it bounces back onto the table. You need the balls in a favorable position for a controlled jump shot as well as both skill and luck to avoid both the pocket and the floor.

At the top, the player decides against making the 5-ball in the corner and drawing the cueball to the left end of the table because of the danger of scratching or because the corner pocket is blocked. An ingenious safety is possible off the pocket point—the cueball goes left, the 5-ball goes right.

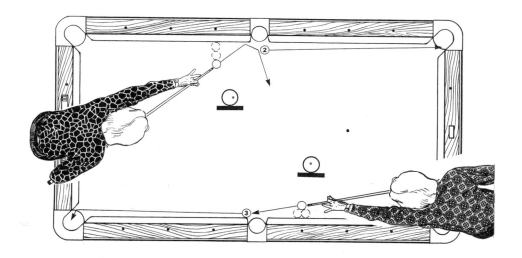

175 Avoiding scratches—II

In some cases you can make a ball in the corner without scratching in the side by going rail first. At the top, the rail-first shot is shown being made—the cueball is two ball widths from the rail at the first diamond from the pocket.

In other cases, the scratch can be avoided by shooting so softly that the object ball just barely reaches the corner. The cueball stops in the jaws without falling in. At the bottom of the diagram is the limiting position—that is, any steeper angle of approach will result in a scratch.

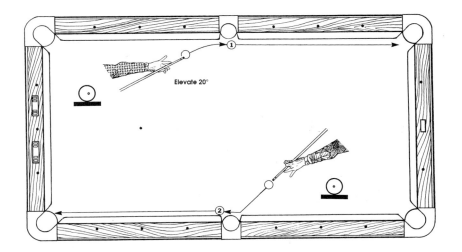

Elevate 20°

176 Avoiding scratches—III

If the angle is too steep for the soft-hit option in the previous diagram, you can try going off the pocket point, as shown at the bottom of this diagram. Making the 2-ball is, admittedly, a low-percentage shot, but the idea can be useful in safety play when balls block other options.

At the top is a massé option to avoid scratching, which I'd never try in a game that meant anything. It's included here for academic completeness.

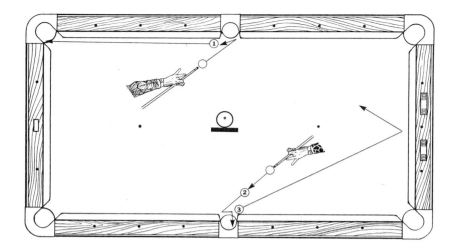

177 Off the point to score

At the top is a well-known challenge shot: make the 1-ball without allowing the cueball to hit the right end rail. It's easy to hit the 1-ball off the point, not so easy to make it in the corner. To make it a cinch, replace the 1-ball with a two- or three-ball combination.

At the bottom is a shot I've never seen in a book, magazine article, on videotape, or in a tournament game. Either the balls never come to rest in this position or nobody thinks of it. An advantage of going off the point to score is that the frozen ball gets bumped to a better place. Even if the balls are arranged so that the 2-ball can be sneaked past the 3-ball and into the pocket with a soft stroke, the off-the-point option might still be better because of the relocation of the 3-ball.

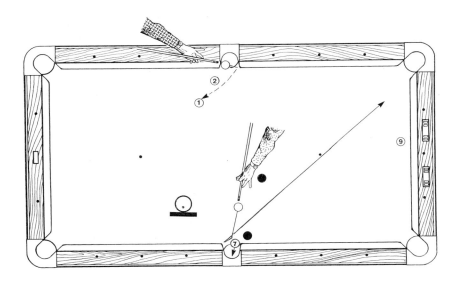

178 Two escapes

The jump shot at the top is fairly easy as jump shots go. Depending on where the other balls are, this could be by far the best way to escape from a hook. (See page 260.)

At the bottom, the problem is to make the 7-ball and get position on the 9-ball at the right end of the table. One way is to hit the 7-ball in such a way that the cueball bounces off the pocket point as shown. The cueball will follow a similar path if the point is hit first, then the ball.

Note that many off-the-pocket-point shots depend on accurate hits as well as good judgment, which is why the cueballs are shown only a foot or two way; at long range, precision hits are much harder to get.

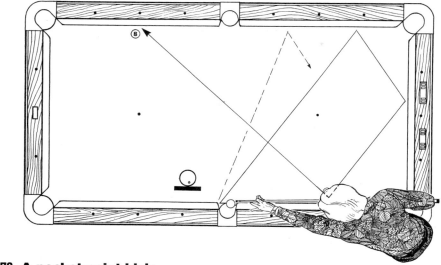

179 A pocket-point kick

You must hit the 8-ball. All direct paths are blocked by intervening balls. Even in the unpromising position shown in the diagram, the goal can be achieved by rebounding off the point to hit three or four more rails. It's not as difficult as it appears, as you will see if you try it ten or fifteen times. The dashed-line path is also fairly predictable.

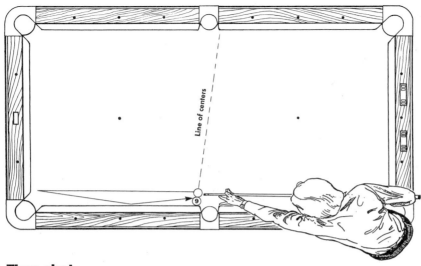

180 Time shot

In a time shot an object ball is deliberately relocated to a spot where it will be hit again by the returning cueball. This lovely example was sent to me by trick-shot inventor and author Sebastien Pauchon of Switzerland. Shoot softly, parallel to the rail, to move the 9-ball about a half inch off the rail. With a little left English, the cueball can be made to come back and delicately cut the 9-ball into the side. This is a setup shot, not for games.

DOUBLE KISSES 13

An underage player in a private club is
discovered by a waiter.
Billard Welt magazine, Berlin, 1913

Schlimme Lage.

Double-kiss, or kiss-back, shots are common in carom games like three-cushion but not so common in pool. Opportunities in pool, however, come up now and then, especially in safety play. Any student of the game who wants to improve should spend some time on the positions given in this section. Most of the examples show the object ball frozen to a cushion and the cueball a short distance away because only then can the required hit be made with confidence. At long range, or when the object ball isn't frozen to a cushion, the outcome of most kiss-back shots becomes dangerously unpredictable. Even then, attempting the kiss might be the best option. In almost all cases, it's best to use a touch of draw, which keeps the kiss-back path straight. Don't use a high ball unless you want the cueball path to curve.

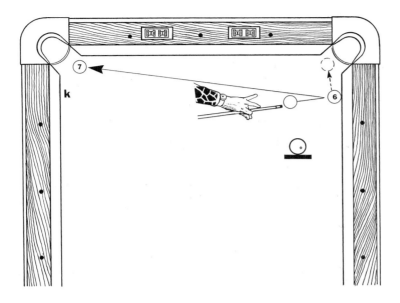

181 **Kiss-across subtleties**

With the 7-ball in the jaws, the 6-ball frozen, and the cueball at point-blank range, making the 7-ball with a direct kiss-back off the 6 is a good bet. The difficulty will come on the next shot, for the 6-ball will hardly have budged. To avoid leaving a bank, add right English to the cueball. Use minimum speed. The transfer of English will nudge the 6-ball to a more favorable position.

If you are a fan of low-percentage trick shots, you can try using low right, kissing back to point *k,* and crossing the table again to pocket the relocated 6-ball.

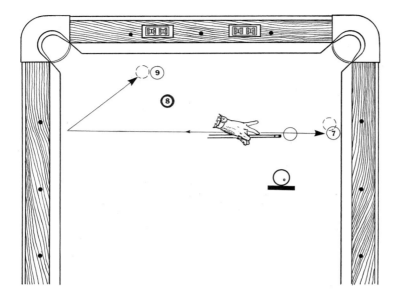

182 Kiss-across safety

How would you play safe in this position? One way is to use low right, hit the 7-ball squarely, and send the cueball across the table to hide behind the 8- and 9-balls. The shot is much harder to judge if the cueball isn't directly opposite the 7-ball or if it is farther away. Sidespin makes it harder to get an accurate hit on *any* shot.

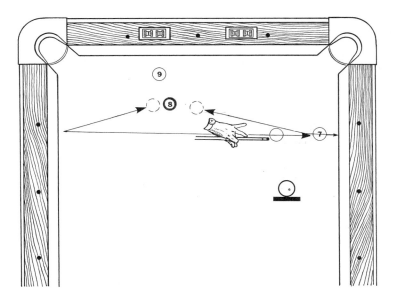

183 Unfrozen double-kiss safety

This is the same as the previous shot except that the 7-ball is a couple of inches off the rail, which makes the outcome enormously more difficult to predict. The problem is that the 7-ball will drift halfway across the table. In the ideal position in the diagram, it's still possible to lay down a safety (see dashed balls). The shot should be listed under "the art of the possible" rather than "the art of the practical," but trying it will show you why kiss-backs are so much harder when the object ball isn't frozen to the cushion.

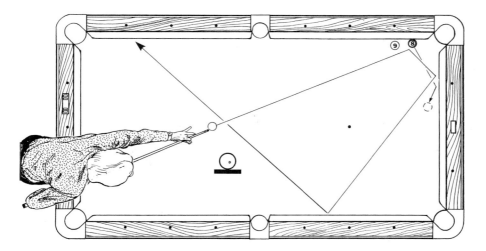

184 Two-rail diagonal safety

Here's a terrible prospect in a game of nine-ball. Or is it? The two- or three-rail safety is not as hard as it looks, as you'll discover if you try it a few times. What else is there? Trying to hit the 8-ball thin leads to disaster.

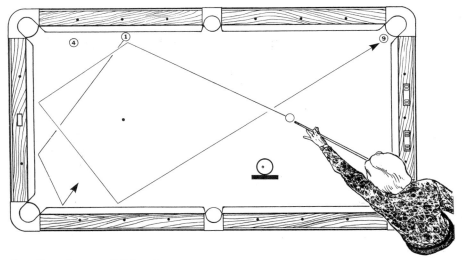

185 Another two-rail kiss

In the previous diagram, the blocker ball almost forces the shooter to try the kiss shot. In the above position, with the upper-left corner pocket blocked and the 9-ball jawed at the other end of the table, how many players would think of the double-kiss shot off the 1-ball? Your guess is as good as mine. There is emotional satisfaction to be gained by imagining yourself winning a game of nine-ball in this fashion, but in real life you will most often use the pattern to send the cue-ball behind blocker balls for a safety.

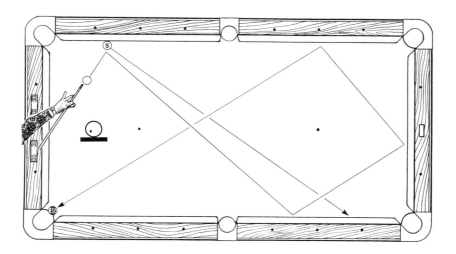

186 Three cushions to score

One reason Efren Reyes became the world's best all-around player is that he spent much of his youth playing rotation in his native Philippines. Here's a position from a game of rotation. The 5-ball is the lowest ball on the table and must be hit first, but if the 15-ball can be pocketed, the shooter gets fifteen points and shoots again. All other balls are omitted for clarity. Because Reyes also plays good three-cushion, he probably would see this kiss-back around-the-table shot.

There are a lot of safety possibilities in shots of this type because by controlling the speed you can bring the cueball to a stop anywhere along the diagrammed path.

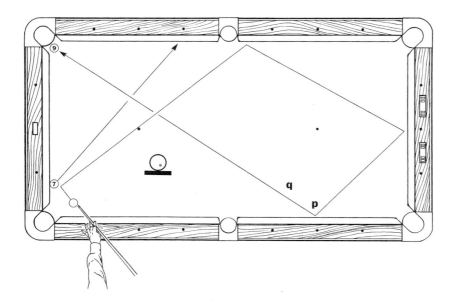

187 Off the end rail

This one is similar to the previous shot, but off the end rail. Balls that rule out more direct paths to the 9-ball are omitted. Again, the pattern will more likely be used to play safe than to pocket a ball. For example, the cueball can be stopped at *p* behind an array of balls at *q*. The technique works best when the object ball is frozen and the cueball is close enough for precision aiming.

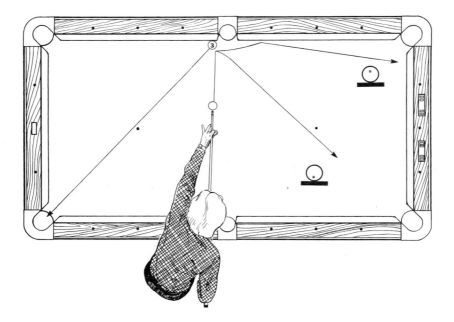

188 Kiss-back paths

A lot can be done in this position by hitting the object ball full enough to get a double kiss. The 3-ball can be banked into the lower-left corner, the cueball can be directed to the lower-right corner, or, with topspin, the cueball can be sent toward the upper-right corner.

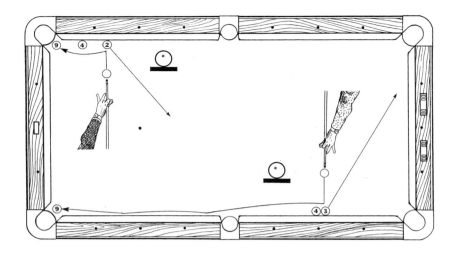

189 Topspin curves

Here are more examples of the curves resulting from topspin. At the upper left, soft speed is the key. At the lower right, only a little more speed is called for. Put these in your trick-shot notebook because they'll probably never come up in a game. On the other hand . . .

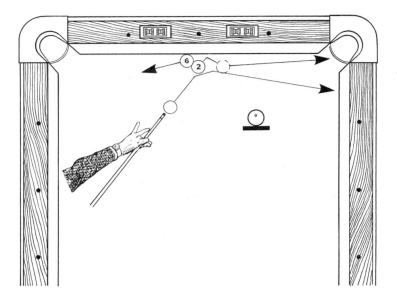

190 The sheepherder shot

This shot reminds me of a border collie herding a sheep into a pen. In an important game, the best bet would probably be a safety, but when playing for fun you might choose to try the double kiss. Because the cueball hits the object ball for the second time after several inches of travel, some players call this a time shot rather than a kiss. Make it once in ten tries and you can take a bow.

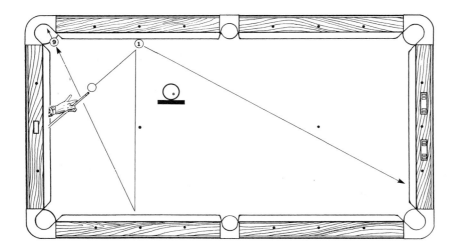

191 Kiss-across surprise

Shot number one in this section is obvious; not so obvious is the kiss-across pattern in this position. The shot can also be made rail first, as was shown in Section 8, Diagram 117.

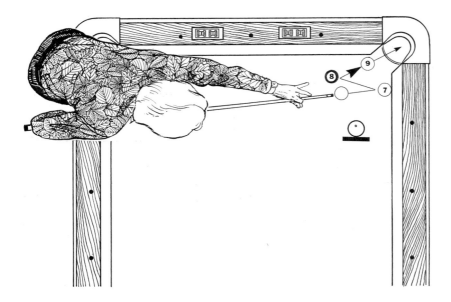

192 **Kiss forward**

In François Mingaud's 1827 book on trick shots, *Noble Jeu de Billard,* is this brilliant idea, which I call the kiss-forward shot. If the cueball has topspin to begin with, the spin will still be there by the time it kisses back from the 7-ball and hits the 8-ball. I'm waiting for a chance to pull this off in a game. Mingaud, a French infantry captain who is credited with inventing the leather cue tip, became a renowned exhibition player in Europe. Because nobody else at the time could spin the cueball the way he could, some thought he was receiving power from the Dark Side.

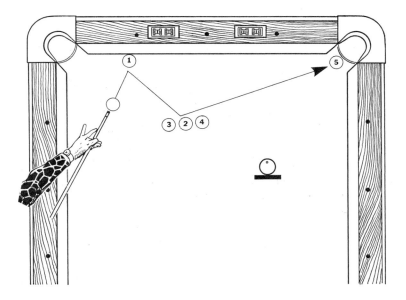

193 Diagonal kiss forward

Here is another application of the kiss-forward concept. The shot can be made by caroming off any one of the three balls.

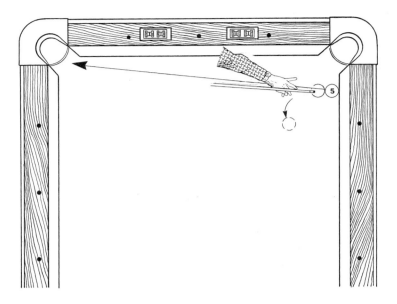

194 The *Hustler* bank

At the beginning of the movie *The Hustler,* Paul Newman, who in real life can hardly make a ball, fleeced the yokels with this shot, now known as the *Hustler* bank. The 5-ball is frozen to the rail and the cueball is frozen to the 5. The line of centers of the two balls forms a right angle with the rail. Elevate the cue slightly, hit the cueball as high as possible without miscuing, and cut the 5-ball just a hair. Let the tip of the cue rise after the hit to avoid fouling the 5 as it rebounds off the cushion. One possible path for the cueball is shown by the dashed line. High-speed photography has shown that the shot is sometimes legal, sometimes foul.

Kraft=Transmiſſion (Uebertragung).

Upsetting a waiter with a tray was a common cartoon theme a hundred years ago.

Courtesy Heinrich Weingartner, Weingartner Billiard Museum

Going rail first to a ball near a rail and caroming back to the same rail—that's a ticky, a common shot in both pool and billiards. The basic pattern in the first diagram is known to almost every player past the beginner stage, but a few of the variations will be new to all but the best-informed veterans.

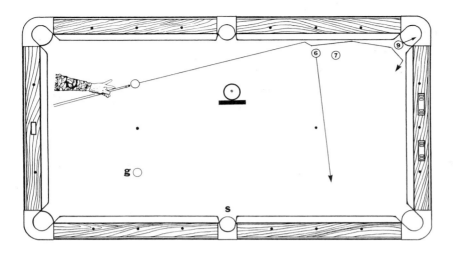

195 The primary pattern

The best chance here to make the 9-ball is to hit the rail first, then the 6-ball, then another rail, and finally the 9-ball. Use very slow speed. If the cueball hits the 6-ball very thin, it may not get back to the rail, but that is almost impossible when the gap between the 6-ball is one ball width or less. The shot as diagrammed is not easy, for the tendency is to hit too much of the 6-ball. If the gap is three or four inches, the shot is much easier. It is also easier from cueball position *g* because rolling topspin acts to keep the cueball close to the rail.

Note that a ball on the lip of the lower side pocket, *s,* can be approached with the ticky pattern by adding more speed.

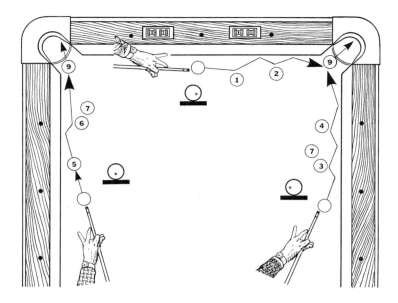

196 Variations

Here are three variations on the main theme. At the left, an object ball is sent on the ticky path. At the top, the cueball caroms off a ball to the rail, which is probably easier than the combination. At the right is the rare double ticky; most players would play safe here without noticing the resource hidden in the position.

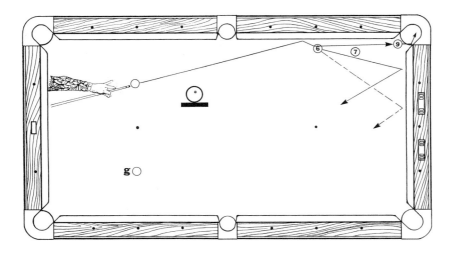

197 **The follow ticky**

The combination is tough, and so is the standard ticky because the 6-ball is less than a ball width from the rail. There is a way out: Hit the rail well before the 6-ball and try to hit the 6 so full that the cueball will follow through in a straight line to the 9-ball. When struck properly, the 6-ball will follow the path indicated by the solid line. From the more favorable cueball position *g,* the 6-ball will follow the dashed line.

The follow ticky is deceptively difficult if you've never tried it. Place the 6-ball two chalk widths from the cushion and see if you can make the 9-ball in your first five attempts from either starting point.

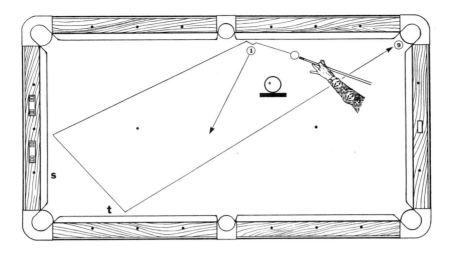

198 Around the table

If there are no balls in the way, a good choice for pocketing the 9-ball is to go off the left side of the 1-ball to points *s* and *t* and back to the upper-right corner. If there are logs in the road in the form of blocker balls, the around-the-table ticky can be tried. It's easy to come close to making the 9-ball with the ticky pattern but not so easy to actually make it, which means that the idea will be of most use in safety play.

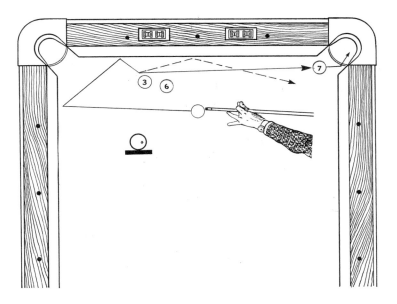

199 Two rails first

Billiard players call this a backup ticky. Aiming closer to the corner pocket with little or no English runs the risk of caroming too sharply off the 3-ball as shown by the dashed line. In this particular position, your chances of pocketing the 9-ball are increased by using right English and aiming as shown—the cueball will rebound off the second rail and hit the 3-ball at a more favorable angle.

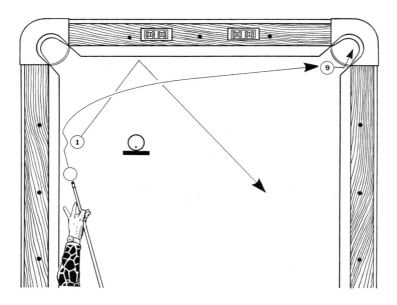

200 The draw ticky

Here's one that even a lot of three-cushion players don't know. Assume that blocker balls prevent a direct carom off the right side of the 1-ball to the 9-ball. The 9-ball can be made by hitting the rail first with heavy draw. The cueball is slowed down by the full hit on the 1-ball, which enables the backspin to curve the path of the cueball dramatically. The thickness of the hit required can be seen by the path of the 1-ball.

To get the hang of it, place the 1-ball a single ball width from the rail; the cueball is one chalk width from the rail. You won't make it the first time you try.

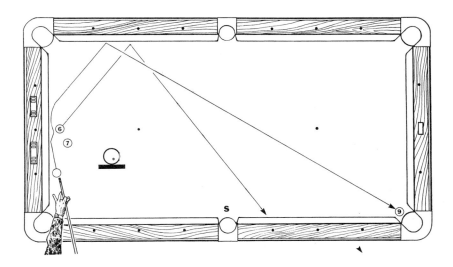

201 Long diagonal draw

The 6-ball is two chalk widths from the rail, the cueball one chalk width. Hitting the rail just before the 6 with low right English will send the two balls diagonally across the table approximately as shown.

With simple running English (high right), and a thinner hit, it is possible to make a ball that is in front of the lower side pocket *s*.

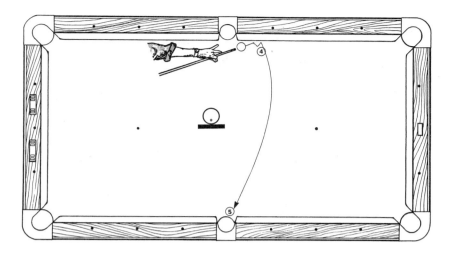

202 The "impossible" ticky

I've rolled up my sleeve to show you a shot that looks like an hallucination. Believe it or not, the ticky pattern with extreme draw can be used to curve the cue-ball path across the table to make the 5-ball. It would make no sense to try this in a game, but if you have a good draw stroke you might add it to your trick-shot show.

An antique cigar box illustration now available as a note card.

Courtesy New Deco, Inc.

When a ball hits a rail, it sinks into the rubber. The depression can be as deep as a quarter of an inch on a hard stroke, which opens the door to a group of shots I call sink-ins. Some are easy; some aren't. They can save the day in escaping from hooks and in creating problems for your contemptible and loathsome opponent.

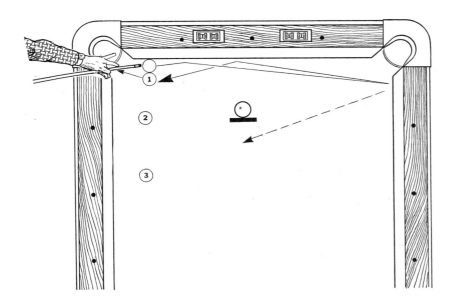

203 An easy one

This easy three-cushion-first double-the-rail shot is possible because the cueball sinks into the rubber to escape from behind the 1-ball. With more left sidespin, the same pattern can be used to hit the 2-ball. No English or running (right) English will send the cueball along the dashed line to hit the 3-ball.

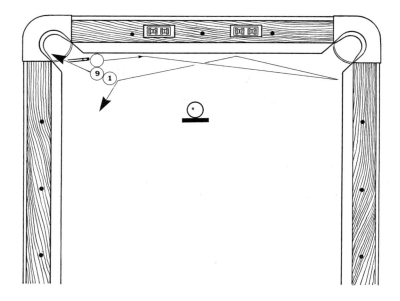

204 An even easier one

Many of the shots diagrammed in this book are tough even for advanced play-ers. To counterbalance that, here's one so easy that you can teach it to tiny children. They may be so pleased at making a reverse-English, double-the-rail combination shot that they will become captivated by the game and unfit for any other activity.

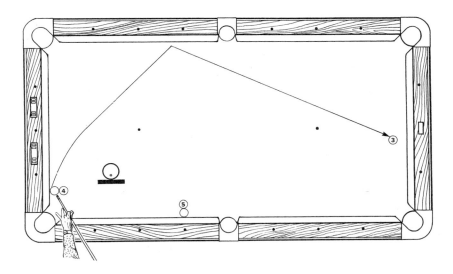

205 The draw curve

Shooting into the rail with draw makes the cueball path curve. Here you not only escape without hitting the 4-ball by compressing the rubber, you hit the 3-ball at the other end of the table. The 3-ball, incidentally, is a ball width from the right end rail, making it a big target for the player trying to escape from the hook. When laying down a safety, try not to leave the target ball close to a rail.

Note the second cueball trapped behind the 5-ball. By using the sink-in technique, from this position you can hit a second ball no matter where it is on the table. In some cases you will need to use two or three rails.

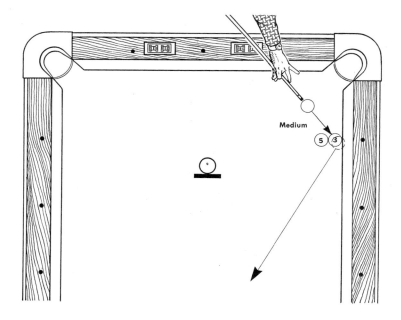

206 First trick shot

The first trick shot I learned as a lad was a sink-in. Place the balls as shown and announce that you will make the 3-ball in the diagonally opposite corner pocket without touching or moving the 5-ball. Point out that the 3-ball, one would think, can only go along the rail if the 5-ball is to remain in place. The deed is done by hitting the 3-ball full in the face with enough force to compress the rubber. As you can see from the location of the dashed ball, the cueball easily clears the 5-ball. That part is easy; skill is needed to actually pocket the ball in the corner, but it becomes easier the more often you try it. Coming close is no problem at all.

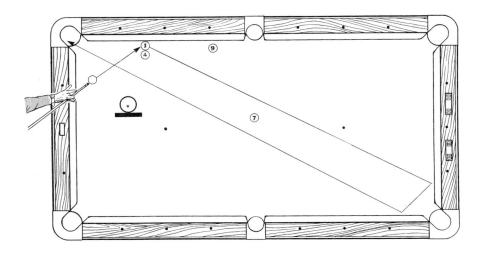

207 Around the table

In the game of one-pocket, each player is assigned a corner pocket. The first to make eight balls in his or her pocket wins. If yours is at the upper left, the around-the-table sink-in shot is a tempting choice, depending on the position of the other balls. With the correct speed, the 1-ball, if it doesn't go in, will come to rest near your pocket.

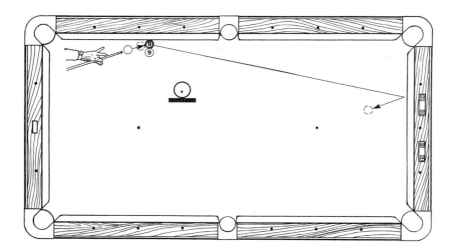

208 Simple safety

Because the cueball is close to the 8-ball, you can shoot a soft stop shot and leave your opponent in a terrible place. Adjust the speed so the 8-ball doesn't stop near the right end rail, thus presenting the smallest possible target.

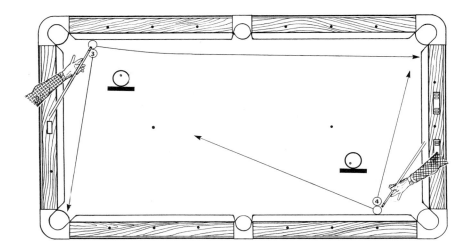

209 Sink in to score

At the upper left, there are two ways to make the 3-ball in the lower-left corner pocket. One is by shooting in the direction opposite of the one shown, throwing the 3-ball. The other is to bridge over the 3-ball, aim into the cushion, and hit the cueball as high as possible to avoid a foul. The choice depends on where you want the cueball to go.

At the lower right, the cueball and the 4-ball are a full diamond away from the end rail. The shot can be made by aiming as shown. It's a hard shot to judge because the direction the 4-ball takes is directly related to how hard you shoot. The more speed you use, the deeper the cueball sinks into the rail, and the thinner is the hit on the 4-ball.

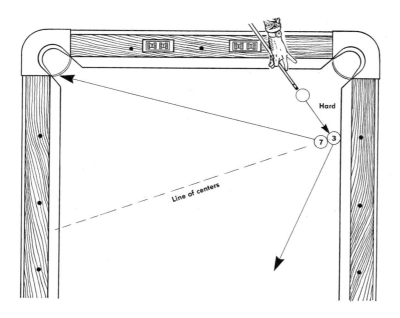

210 The limiting position

As unlikely as it may seem, the 7-ball can be made in the upper-left corner pocket. You have to shoot hard and the line of centers can't be more steeply angled.

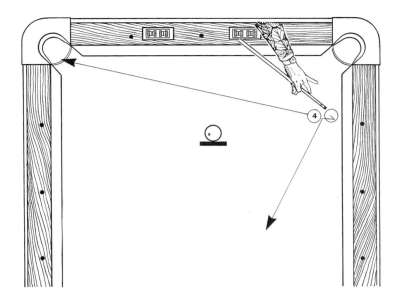

211 Rail first

The cueball is not frozen to the rail. Choosing the right aiming line to make the 4-ball takes practice because you have to learn to judge how deeply the cueball will sink into the rail at various speeds.

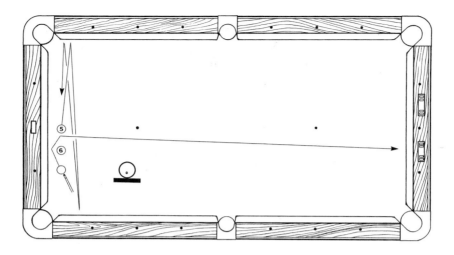

212 A great escape

There is a gap of one ball width between the cushion and the 6-ball. Can the cueball be squeezed through to hit the 5-ball and avoid a foul? Yes. One possible way to return the safety is shown in the diagram, but that is admittedly arbitrary. The lesson to learn is that the cueball can be forced through holes that look too small at first glance.

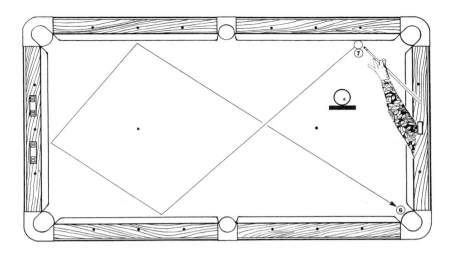

213 Richie's Shot

This was one of the late Richie Florence's favorite exhibition shots. To make it you have to be able to follow straight through to avoid fouling the 7-ball with your cue, and you have to shoot hard, not only to get around the table but to avoid moving the 7-ball.

This scene was repeated almost daily at Palace Billiards, San Francisco,
in the 1970s.

Photo by John Grissim

It's illegal to make the cueball jump by golfing it off the cloth with a low hit. Raising the back of the cue, however, and striking the cueball a downward blow to get it airborne is quite all right. Skilled players these days routinely escape from hooks by jumping the cueball over blocking balls. The technique is much easier with a special tool designed for the job, the jump cue. Jump cues are shorter than normal cues and are balanced toward the front to make them more comfortable to handle when steeply elevated. The most important difference is that they are much lighter.

Pool cues normally weigh between 17 and 21 ounces and are from 54 to 59 inches long, while jump cues weigh as little as 8 ounces and can be as short as 40 inches. The light weight is to enable the cue to rebound quickly from the 6-ounce cueball. The jump cue's hard tip also facilitates a quick rebound. Some players can make the cueball jump over other balls by using just the shaft of a two-piece cue.

At angles of elevation greater than, say, 45 degrees, it is less awkward to grip the cue from underneath so it can be held close to the face for aiming. The stroke then becomes a motion similar to throwing a dart. (See page 284.)

Experimentation in Japan by Kengo Hitomi using an 8.5-ounce jump cue called the Lucasi L-2000JC suggests that if the downward angle of the cue is 30 degrees, the cueball leaves the table at an angle of 20 degrees, while a cue angle of 67 degrees results in a cueball jump angle of about 50 degrees. How high the cueball rises depends on the force of the blow. While it is possible to put backspin and even sidespin on a jumped cueball with a steeply elevated cue, controlling the cueball with precision is impossible. The main risk is that the cueball will come to rest on the floor instead of the table.

A jump cue in the right hands renders many safeties harmless, which greatly affects the character of the game. For that reason, jump cues are barred in some leagues and tournaments. The shots in this section are possible with a normal cue.

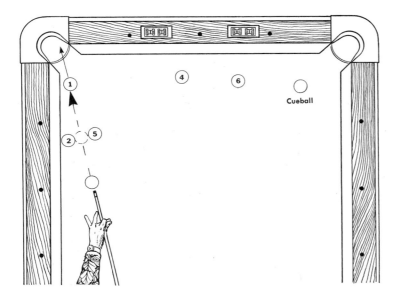

214 Easy and hard

At the left, the challenge is to shoot through a gap that is precisely the width of the cueball. Use the cueball to position the 2-ball and the 5-ball, then place the cueball as shown in the diagram. The shot is impossible with a level cue, and child's play with the cue elevated 10 degrees or so.

At the top right, the 4-ball is straight in, but the 6-ball is in the way. It is possible to jump the cueball all the way over the 6-ball to make the 4-ball, but only very good players can do it consistently with a normal cue.

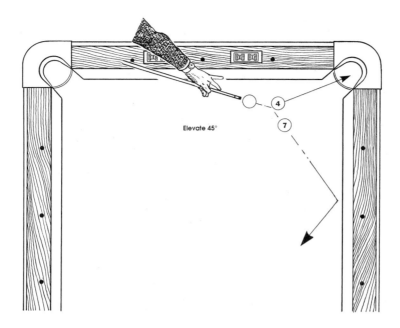

Elevate 45°

215 Second-ball jump

It's not hard to jump over a full ball if you hit another ball first. The cueball is ramped upward if it is still rising when it hits the first ball. In the diagram, the margin of error for making the 4-ball is large, making it feasible to get the cueball to the other end of the table by jumping over the 7-ball. Less speed and less elevation are required if the cueball is jumping over less than a full ball.

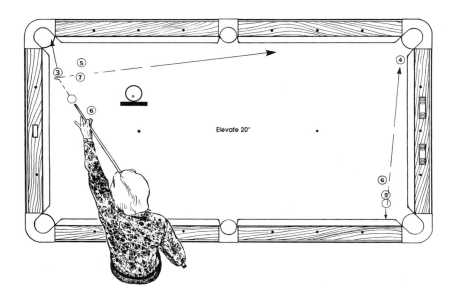

216 Ball-rail jump

At the left, the cueball can pocket the 3-ball and get to the other end of the table by jumping off the nose of the cushion. The shot is not as hard as it looks in the given position, but it is not worth trying if the cueball is several feet farther away. Unless the cueball is less than a foot from the first ball, the risk of jumping off the table is too great.

How would you escape from the safety at the right? Although the cueball is only about three inches from the cushion, it is possible to bridge over the 5-ball, hit down on the cueball, bounce off the nose of the cushion, and jump over the 5-ball and 6-ball to pocket the 4-ball. An elevation of at least 50 degrees is required.

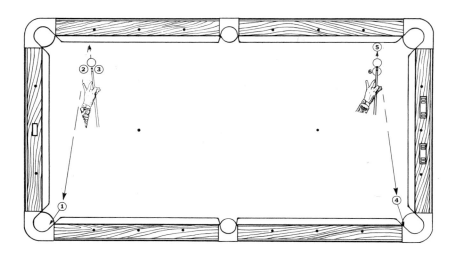

217 Easier and harder

The jump bank at the left is easier than the last shot because the cueball is a few inches farther from the rail and it is easier to strike the cueball. A good player can make it at least three times out of four.

The jump bank at the right is more difficult because the cueball must kiss back off a frozen ball. This is a harder shot, but it's still possible. Don't bet against it. You should never, of course, bet against somebody else's proposition.

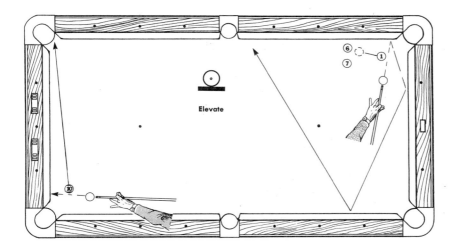

Elevate

218 The thin-hit jump

Willie Jopling, writing in *Billiards Digest* magazine, explained how the 10-ball can be cut in even though it seems impossible to avoid the immediate scratch. The secret is to jump the cueball so that it contacts the object ball above the equator. Making the 10-ball as drawn is not too likely, but getting it started in the right direction without scratching, which might be useful in the game of one-pocket, is within the reach of intermediate players.

At the right is another application of the thin-hit jump shot. The cueball banks three rails without scratching while the 1-ball moves slowly to the left for a safety.

The danger in both shots is that you will (*a*) scratch anyway, and (*b*) jump off the table.

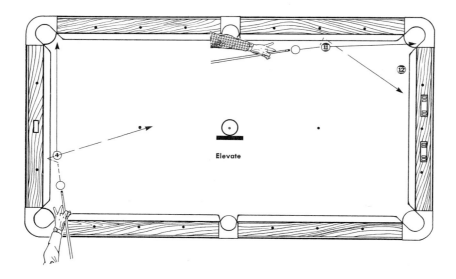

219 Falling off the ledge

At the left, the 4-ball is almost, but not quite, straight in. Can you make the 4-ball and at the same time get the cueball down the table? Because the 4-ball is close to the rail and the cueball is only ten inches or so away, the door is open for a clever positional play. Elevate the butt of the cue (the amount depends on the circumstances), shoot down at the 4-ball, and try to get the cueball to land on top of the rubber. If you succeed, the cueball will fall off the nose of the cushion and roll toward the center of the table.

The value of the shot is shown at the upper right. The way the balls are located makes it very hard to make the 11-ball and get position on the 12-ball. Position is achieved with the jump-onto-the-rail shot.

The trick is to avoid hitting anything but the cushion. It's a foul if the cueball touches wood. The best action results not when the cueball lands completely on top of the rubber, but rather when the edge of the cueball hits the nose of the cushion on its way down.

You'll put a lot of cueballs on the floor practicing this one.

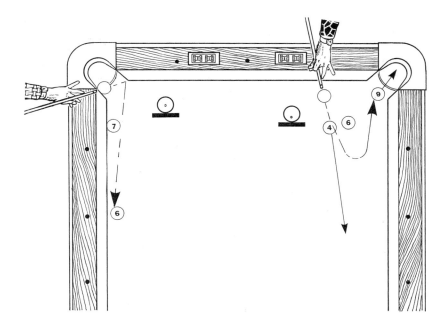

220 The point jump and the jump draw

On the left, escaping the hook with a jump off the pocket point is surprisingly easy to do consistently. I'm still waiting for the position to come up in a game.

The famous jump draw shot is shown on the right. The only way to make the cueball advance beyond the object ball before coming back is to make it leave the cloth. The position is as easy as this tough shot ever is—you are close to the object ball, the 9-ball is a big target, and you can form your bridge on the rail to facilitate a downward blow.

The concept is used for the over-and-under trick shot, explained in *Byrne's Treasury of Trick Shots in Pool and Billiards* (1982), page 9.

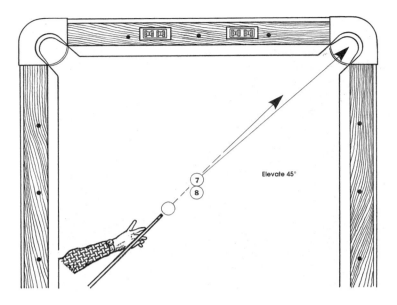

Elevate 45°

221 The frozen spot shot

The 8-ball is on the spot and the 7-ball is frozen directly behind it. With ball in hand, can you make the 7-ball straight into the corner pocket? World trick-shot champion Mike Massey can, and maybe you can, too. Place the cueball as shown, elevate your cue about 45 degrees, and jump the cueball over the edge of the 8-ball onto the top of the 7-ball.

Note that the aiming line is slightly to the left to keep the cueball from fol-lowing the 7-ball into the pocket.

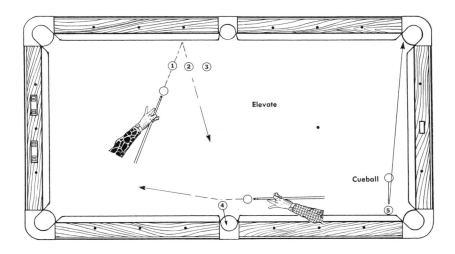

222 Lots of luck

You'll need lots of luck to make these three shots, which are included for amusement purposes only. At the top, the challenge is to bank the 1-ball into the side by making it jump over the 2-ball. Stefano Pelinga, trick-shot champion of Italy, makes it look easy.

At the right is something even worse. Bank the 5-ball. How? With a jump shot. The cueball hits the 5-ball and jumps a foot in the air while the 5-ball passes under it. I've seen Mike Massey do it. I've done it myself when nobody was watching.

At the bottom is an apparently impossible cut shot. According to Willie Jopling, it can be made by jumping the cueball so that it lands on the far side of the 4-ball. I told you up front that you'll need lots of luck.

POCKET POINTS

PARIS LE SOIR.

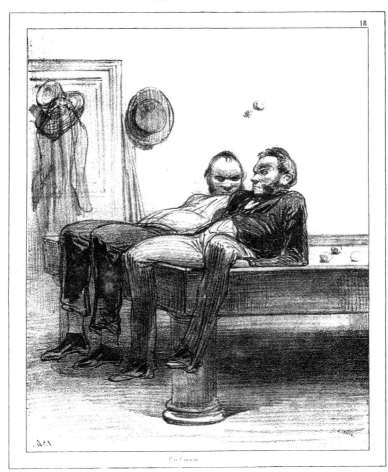

A break in the action.
Courtesy Heinrich
Weingartner,
Weingartner Billiard
Museum

All sorts of surprising things can be done by making use of the pocket points, as demonstrated by the examples in this section. If you find an opportunity in a game to send a cueball or an object ball off a pocket point, don't complain about a miss if you've never practiced the shot. There is a stimulating unpredictability about pocket-point shots because a small change in aim can transform opportunity into catastrophe. Nevertheless, they are sometimes the best, or even the only, way to play safe or escape from a safety.

See also Section 12, "Side Pockets."

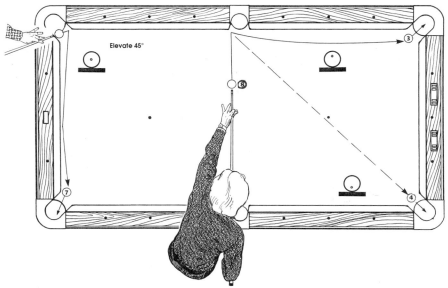

Elevate 45°

223 Point the way

At the left, the shooter is corner hooked, which is to say that the corner of the pocket prevents a direct shot at the object ball. The 7-ball can be hit by banking the cueball off the right end rail or by banking three rails, but those avenues might be blocked by other balls. The diagrammed path is a very good alternative. I find it best to elevate the cue to 45 degrees or so and shoot softly in order to slide the cueball into the pocket point, thus eliminating the hard-to-judge topspin curve.

In the middle of the table, the 8-ball blocks direct shots at the jawed 3-ball and 4-ball. Making the 3-ball off the point is better than a fifty-fifty proposition once you get used to it. Topspin keeps the cueball close to the rail. Making the 4-ball (dashed line) by hitting more of the point is harder but is not a bad choice in the given position.

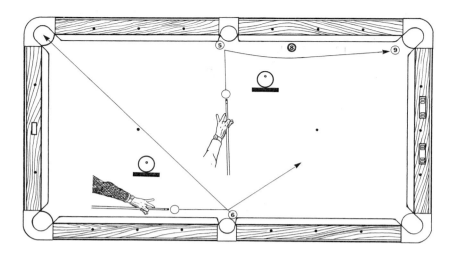

224 **Kiss back off the point**

Here are two examples of kissing back off a ball that is frozen against the point of a side pocket. At the top, notice the way topspin enables the cueball to curve around the 8-ball.

At the bottom, making the 6-ball in the upper-left corner is no cinch, but you should at least be able to come close, which is important in the game of one-pocket.

As is always the case, kiss-back shots are infinitely easier to judge if the object ball is frozen to the rail, not just close to being frozen, and the cueball is close enough for precise aiming.

225 A challenge shot

This invention of mine only works if the pockets aren't too tight. Position the balls as shown at the upper right and announce that you will make both the 1-ball and the 9-ball. Did somebody say it can't be done? Carom the 1-ball off the 9-ball and hit the cueball high. The 9-ball, if all goes according to plan, bounces off the point and moves to the other side of the corner pocket, where the oncoming cueball knocks it in. Shown at the left is the situation after the 1-ball is in the pocket and the cueball is advancing toward the relocated 9-ball.

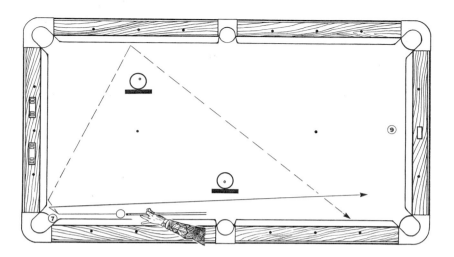

226 **An accidental discovery**

I discovered this move by accident. I was trying to make the 7-ball, which my unlucky opponent had left in the jaws, and get position on the 9-ball by using high right and going two or three rails along the dashed line. Instead, the cue-ball caught the pocket point and went straight down the rail as shown by the solid line. My opponent thought I did it on purpose. When accidents like this happen in crucial matches, it is vital to keep a straight face.

Set up the shot for a friend, block the dashed line with balls, and see if he or she can get position on a ball at the right end of the table. When demonstrating the shot yourself, forget the high right and simply use centerball. Not much speed is needed.

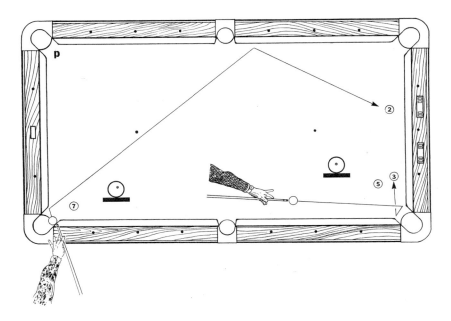

227 Escaping corner hooks

At the lower-left corner, what's the best way to hit the 2-ball at the right end of the table? The 7-ball blocks a one-rail bank. Off the corner point as shown is not as difficult as it looks. With a harder stroke, it's possible to use the same pattern to go all the way around the table to pocket or hit a ball at *p* at the upper-left corner, though that shot is best left to the trick-shot arena.

At the lower right, going off both pocket points to hit the 3-ball is a completely practical idea, but it takes a bit of practice. It's especially useful when the cueball is at the other end of the table and other pathways are blocked.

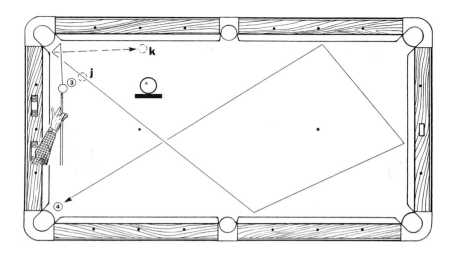

228 Two 2-point shots

Hitting balls at *k* or *j* can be done by hitting both pocket points, as with the shot at the lower right in the previous diagram. It is also possible to go off both points around the table to make or hit a ball in the lower left corner, as shown by the solid line, or to hit a ball that is located anywhere along that line. Better announce your intentions in advance or everybody in the room will think you got lucky.

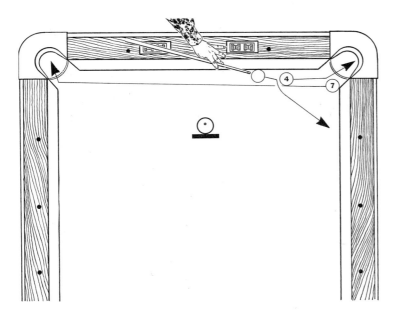

229 A kiss-back dream bank

You are dreaming about a game of one-pocket. Your pocket is at the left, your smug opponent's at the right. You each need to make one more ball to win. If you make a ball in each pocket with one stroke, you still win. Because the 7-ball is in a certain exact spot, you can make the 4-ball in your opponent's pocket by caroming it off the 7-ball, which banks off the point into your pocket for a stunning victory followed by your opponent going outside to throw himself under a bus.

Permit me to place the balls and I'll make this shot once in five tries.

The adventures of all-around athlete Frank Merriwell were chronicled in *Tip Top Weekly* in the 1890s. Here he silences a billiard room braggart with a massé shot.

From the Byrne Collection

In a strict technical sense, every shot is a massé shot unless the cue is exactly level and hits the cueball precisely on the vertical axis without a trace of sidespin. If the cueball path curves even slightly because of sidespin and a downward hit, it is a massé shot. The big massés that make the cueball travel in weird, looping paths are best left to exhibition players. Executing those eye-popping showstoppers requires a short stiff, heavy cue, coaching from an expert, and a table to practice them on.

Little massés, on the other hand, don't require a special cue or an explosive stroke. When opportunities for them come up, the great majority of players pass them by. Either they don't see them, or they think they are too hard. Little massés, the kind that are worth trying in games, aren't easy, but with a bit of knowledge and practice, they are no harder than, say, an off-angle bank. Massés should be considered in games when the cueball is within an inch or two of the object ball; at greater distances controlling the curve is usually too hard. It also helps if the final target is large—a ball in the jaws, for example, or a safety zone behind a group of balls.

A geometric method of aiming massé shots was worked out in 1835 by physicist Gaspard-Gustave Coriolis and then forgotten for a century and a half. It was demonstrated on *Byrne's Standard Video of Pool, Volume II* and explained in detail in *Byrne's Advanced Technique in Pool and Billiards* (1990). To save you the trouble of running to your bookshelf for the book or tape, here is a condensed description:

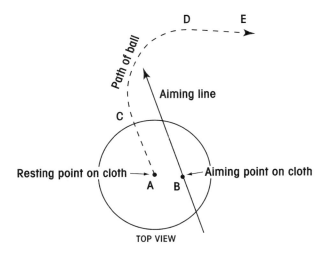

TOP VIEW

230 The geometry of massé shots

The circle in this diagram is the cueball as viewed from directly overhead. Point *A* is where the cueball rests on the cloth. Assume that *AC* is the direction you want the cueball to take initially and *DE* the desired final direction. Because you want the cueball to curve to the right, you must use right English. Start with the cue level, aiming as shown by the solid arrow labeled "Aiming line," which is parallel to *AC*. Raise the cue to about 67 degrees and aim through the cueball at a point on the cloth, *B,* so that *AB* is parallel to *DE*. It's up to you to bring the cue down on the cueball at the correct speed, for the harder you hit it, the farther out it will go before it curves.

While it is not necessary to understand the physics behind this aiming method—almost all top players rely on simple judgment based on practice and most have never heard of Coriolis—I find keeping the geometry in mind very helpful for the relatively soft massés discussed in this section.

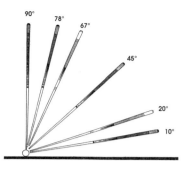

231 Degrees of elevation

In this diagram are a few common degrees of elevation. Halfway between 45 degrees and 90 degrees is 67.5 degrees, rounded off here to 67 degrees. Halfway between 67.5 and 90 is 78.75 degrees, rounded off here to 78 degrees. You aren't limited to these angles, but they work for many small massés.

A vertical cue is used for straight draw action—no curve is involved unless you hit an object ball or a rail at an angle.

Some players don't change their grip hands when they raise the cue for a downward blow, no matter how great the angle. Others hold the cue from underneath when the angle gets greater than 40 or 50 degrees. Most of the shots in this section require a deft and accurate stroke rather than power, so for the steep angles I recommend the underhand grip using the pads of the thumb and first two fingers and a motion similar to throwing a dart.

When practicing massés, chalk up after every try to minimize the miscues.

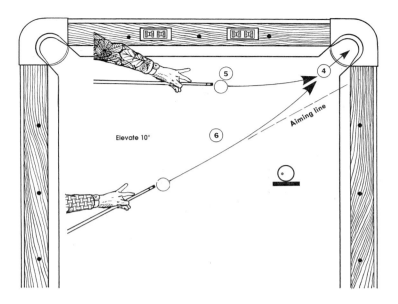

Elevate 10°

Aiming line

232 Two swerves

Here are two shots that require a slightly curved cueball path that will carry the cueball around the edges of blocking balls and into a ball in the jaws of the corner pocket, a very large target. Both require only a slight elevation of the cue, around 10 degrees. At the top, aim to barely miss the 5-ball and use a soft stroke. Without slow speed, the cueball will reach the rail before it has a chance to curve. At the bottom, more speed is required to make sure the cueball gets past the 6-ball before it curves to the left.

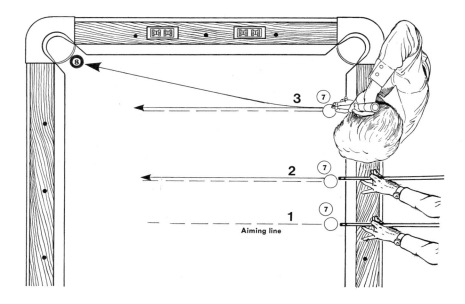

233 **Three-step aiming**

Position 3 at the top requires the cueball to curve around the 7-ball, cross the table, and curve into the jawed 8-ball. The aiming technique can be broken into three parts. First, use a level cue and aim the cueball to barely miss the edge of the 7-ball, as shown in position 1. Second, move the level cue to the right, keeping it parallel with the original aiming line, as shown in position 2. Finally, raise the cue, and aim down through the ball at a point that will provide the correct amount of curve as explained in the introduction to this section. Shoot just hard enough to make the 8-ball, not so hard that a perfect hit will cause the cueball to follow the 8-ball into the pocket.

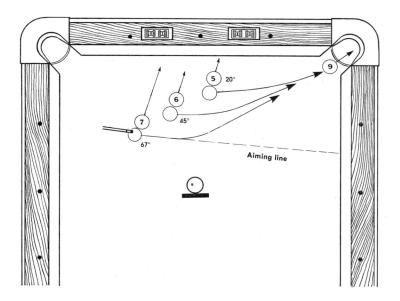

234 Three practice shots

In each of the three shots, the ball close to the cueball must be hit first. Note how the degree of elevation increases along with the necessary curve. Making the 9-ball off the 7-ball requires the cueball to curve so sharply that I would think twice before trying it in a game, unless a miss would result in a safety.

REMINDER: Shoot just hard enough to make the shot. For best results, the object ball should be hit so thin that it only moves a few inches.

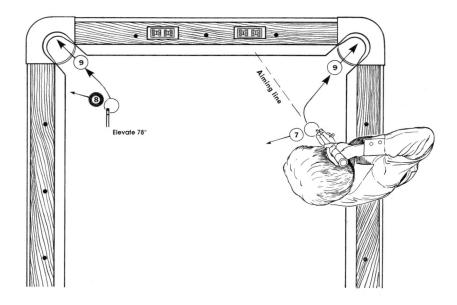

Elevate 78°

Aiming line

235 **Two practical massés**

These are shots that cry out for massés. If you've put in some practice time, you should approach them with confidence. Shame on you if you play safe instead. Chalk up and shoot softly.

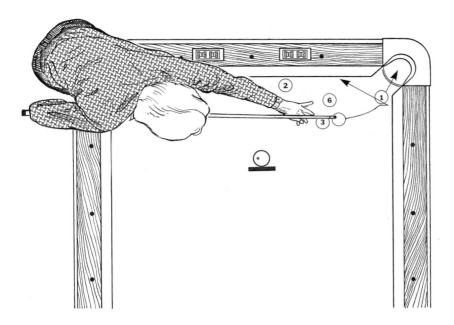

236 Inside forced massé

We've all faced shots like this. Making the 1-ball and getting position on the 2-ball would be easy with a thin hit and left-hand English if you didn't have to shoot over the three-ball. Because the 3-ball forces you to elevate the cue, you must aim to miss the 3-ball by an inch or two, relying on the massé curve to bring the cueball to left. This is easy once you get used to it.

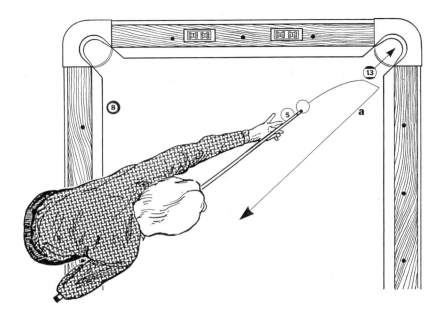

237 Outside forced massé

Here's another shot in which you are forced to play a massé in order to make the 13-ball and get position on the 8-ball. It's practical because there is a large margin of error. Top players occasionally try massés of this type even when the object ball is six inches or so away from the pocket.

Massés of this type can also be used to lightly separate a cluster at point *a*.

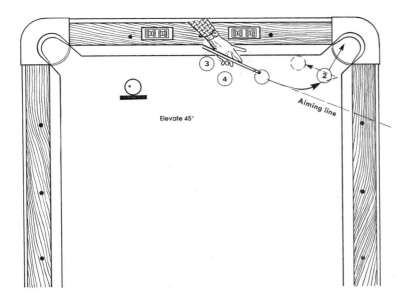

Elevate 45°

Aiming line

238 **Reverse position**

It would be nice if you could cut a ball to the left and make the cueball go left as well. You can do it with massé. In the diagram, cutting the 2-ball in with a level cue will send the cueball to the right and position on the 3-ball would be lost. Aiming to miss as shown with a sharp massé curve can pocket the 2-ball and keep the 3-ball in sight. With luck, the cueball might end up in the position of the dashed ball, a very emotionally satisfying result. The shot is not easy, but it's worth a try if a precise hit on the 2-ball is not required, as is the case here.

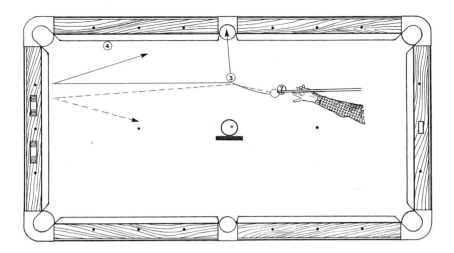

239 Swerve position

If it weren't for the 7-ball, it would be easy to cut the 3-ball in the side with right English and get position on the 4-ball. The 7-ball forces you to use an elevated cue. With no sidespin, the cueball will travel along the path shown by the dashed line. Using right English to get position on the 4-ball makes the cueball curve to the right on its way to the 3-ball. Allow for the curve by aiming to miss the 3-ball by about an inch. There is enough margin of error in making the 3-ball to make the shot a risk worth taking.

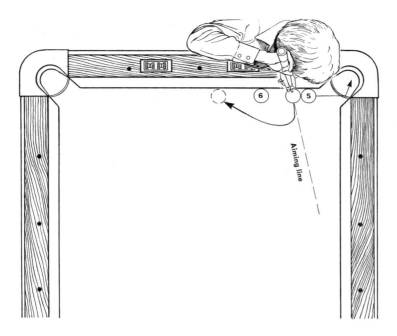

Aiming line

240 U-turn position

All three balls are frozen to the rail. If the left-hand pocket is blocked, or if the game is one-pocket and you must make both balls in the right-hand pocket, a massé shot is the answer to your prayers. I sometimes practice this shot just for the fun of it. Use a nearly vertical cue. If the cueball comes back on the wrong side of the 6-ball, aim more toward the 5-ball.

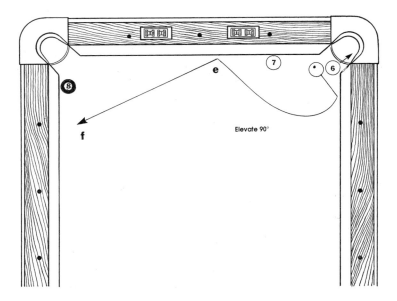

Elevate 90°

241 U-turn extended

Use a fully elevated cue and no sidespin. After the cueball cuts in the 6-ball, it will proceed in a straight line to the rail. The backspin takes after the cueball rebounds from the rail. Depending on the amount of force used, the cueball stops near *e* for position on the 7-ball, or near *f* for position on the 8-ball. This one is for advanced players only.

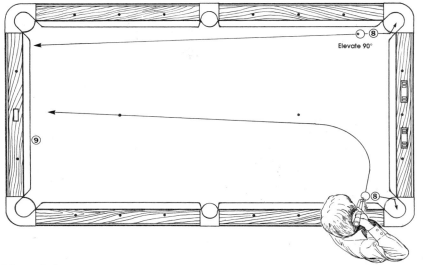

Elevate 90°

242 Massé draw

With a full massé, it's easy to draw a ball the length of the table.

At the top, draw with a level cue is difficult because the gap is small and a foul is likely. With a vertical cue, the double hit is avoided and a soft stroke puts plenty of backspin on the cueball. By "easy," I mean it can be done fairly consistently by an average player who puts in some practice time. Get your cue out of the way in a hurry.

At the bottom, the gap is so small that the cueball must be directed away from the object ball to avoid a foul. The angle of elevation is 5 or 10 degrees less than 90. Because the cueball must curve to the left to get position on the 9-ball, hit the cueball left of center as you look down on it from above.

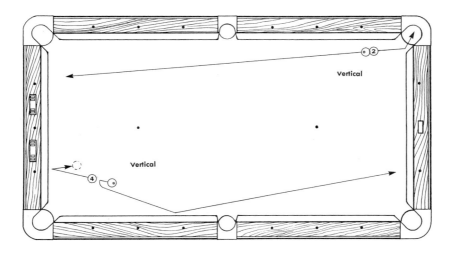

243 **Frozen massé**

At the top, the cueball is frozen to the 2-ball. A full massé without sidespin will send the cueball the length of the table for position.

At the bottom is a safety play. Drawing the cueball to the right-hand end rail with a level cue puts too much speed on the 4-ball. To keep the 4-ball from moving too much, use a full massé. If done correctly, the cueball will be slowing down and about to change direction when it lightly kisses the 4-ball. This is an idea to keep in mind if you have a good massé touch. With the balls a foot from the lower rail, a freehand bridge is required: Suspend your bridge hand about four inches above the cueball. Lean toward the balls and press your elbow to the side of your body to steady your forearm as much as possible.

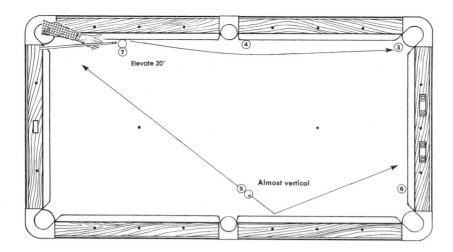

Elevate 20°

Almost vertical

244 Frozen rail swerve

The shot at the top is not as hard as it looks. The 7-ball prevents a normal curve-around-the-blocker shot. Elevate the cue about 20 degrees, use left English, and shoot into the rail to avoid hitting the 7-ball. With any luck at all the cueball will curve around the 4-ball to make the 3-ball.

The frozen draw shot at the bottom is similar to the top shot in the previous diagram but much more difficult because the object ball is far from the pocket. The goal is to draw back for one-rail position on the 6-ball. You'll find out when using a full massé that pocketing the 5-ball is no cinch. It's hard to aim accurately with a steep angle of elevation. Furthermore, even the slightest sidespin on the cueball will throw the 5-ball off line.

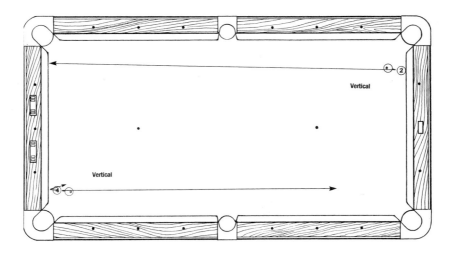

245 Kiss-back massé

At the top, the 2-ball is frozen to the rail and you have decided to kiss back to the other end of the table for a safe leave. The gap is so small that a level cue will almost certainly result in a miscue. A full massé is the way to go. Because of the kiss-back effect, a very soft stroke is all that's required for lively action on the cueball.

It's not necessary for the object ball to be frozen, but when it isn't, it's harder to judge the paths of the two balls. At the bottom, the 4-ball will bounce off the rail to give the cueball a boost before the massé action takes effect.

Because you don't need much force on either of these shots, you can use a stroke only three or four inches long. Use a freehand bridge (the fingertips don't touch the cloth), pressing your forearm against your body for solidity and leaning forward to position the tip of the cue.

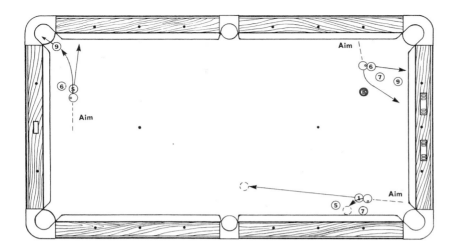

246 The push curve

In these three shots, the cueball is frozen to an object ball. You can exploit the fact that the cueball will move forward before curving. A soft stroke is used and an elevation of about 60 degrees.

At the upper left, the cueball can get around the 6-ball to make the 9-ball with massé action off the 5-ball.

At the upper right, the cueball can be curved around the 7-ball and 9-ball to leave your opponent no shot on the 6-ball.

At the lower right, a soft massé stroke will bury the cueball behind the 5-ball for a safety.

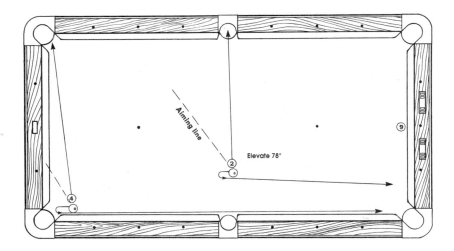

Aiming line

Elevate 78°

247 Backward position

With a massé, the cueball can be made to stop on a dime and reverse direction. Examine the position near the side pocket. The problem is to pocket the 2-ball in the upper side pocket and get position on the 9-ball at the right end rail. A massé gets the job done. Use a short freehand bridge and lean forward to position the tip of the cue. The indicated aiming line will give the 2-ball enough speed to reach the pocket. It's a beautiful thing to see the cueball start out in one direction and then turn around to go in another.

At the lower left is the same shot, but positioned so that it seems impossible to cut the 4-ball into the upper-left corner pocket without scratching. If you get good massé action, the cueball will enter the jaws of the pocket before changing course and speeding to the other end of the table for position.

Groom and chalk your tip well before trying any massé shot.

Do not try this without coaching from a trained professional. Tip-toeing up and down your cue is a method of humiliating a defeated opponent.

Courtesy Heinrich Weingartner, Weingartner Billiard Museum

There are hundreds of geometric, numeric, and proportional systems to help players find the correct line of aim when the cueball has to be banked off one or more rails. Systems are especially useful in three-cushion billiards, where the cueball must hit at least three rails on every shot; they are not nearly as useful in pool. Most top pool players rely on instinct or judgment when escaping from safeties, not on systems. There are even great three-cushion players who don't use systems: American champion Sang Chun Lee, for example, feels that relying on systems interferes with the development of judgment.

Still, a good system can take some of the guesswork out of certain cueball bank shots. Guesswork can't be eliminated entirely, for the line of aim is only one of three variables, the others being speed and spin. The type of rubber and the condition of the balls and the cloth also affect rebound angles.

Systems are often loosely called "diamond systems," even though many of them are not dependent on the inlaid marks on the wooden part of the rails, which a hundred years ago were diamond-shaped.

Many systems are based on the assumption that a table is twice as long as it is wide, which isn't quite true. A full-sized pool table, for example, is said to be $4\frac{1}{2}$ feet wide by 9 feet long. Here's a good trivia question: What is 9 feet long on a pool table? Hardly anybody knows. You might be surprised to learn that nothing of importance or interest is nine feet long on a pool table.

The width of a full-sized table measures $4\frac{1}{2}$ feet (54 inches) from the back of the rubber (where the cloth meets the wood on top of the rail) to the back of the rubber on the opposite side. The cushions are 2 inches wide, so the distance from nose to nose of the cushions is 50 inches. Doubling that gives the length of the table; that is, it is 100 inches from the nose of the cushion at one end to the nose of the cushion at the opposite end. The dimensions aren't fixed, though, because the rubber compresses when hit by a ball. It can also be argued that the playing surface is not 50 by 100 inches because the bottom of the cue-ball never gets closer than half its width to the rail, except when compressing the rubber. Using that approach, the playing surface is 47¾ inches wide by 97¾ inches long. No wonder the various systems aren't perfectly accurate.

In this section, I will explain three systems that are helpful in pool and that don't require adding or subtracting numbers and fractions in your head. They can be applied quickly—so quickly that your opponent may not realize that you are using a system. They work best if you take a minute before the game to determine the characteristics of the table by shooting certain test banks.

For more on banking systems, see *Byrne's New Standard Book of Pool and Billiards* (1998), pages 273–300.

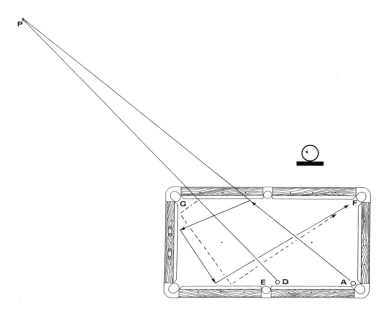

248 Around the table—I

This is a non-numerical version of the so-called corner-five system well known to three-cushion players. Master it and you will be able to bank the cueball around the table off three or more rails with considerable accuracy. The "distant point" method is used to find the correct line of aim. When playing on a table for the first time, a couple of practice banks will locate the distant point.

In the diagram, place a ball in the jaws at *A* and bank the cueball with running English (left) three rails to the upper-right corner pocket, *F*. When you find an aiming line that pockets the cueball at *F*, extend it beyond the table, noting a point on the rug or wall or a nearby table that is roughly ten feet beyond the table. That is point *P*. To nail it down exactly, shoot from *D* until the ball goes in at *F*, then extend that line until it intersects the first one. In practice, though, extending the line from *A* and picking a point between ten and twelve feet away is good enough.

Once you have located *P*, you can bank the cueball three rails to *F* no matter where the cueball is simply by aiming it at *P* with running English. The exception is when the cueball is to the left of the line *EG*, in which case you can't hit the first rail. As the starting point of the cueball moves from *A* to *E*, more sidespin must be used.

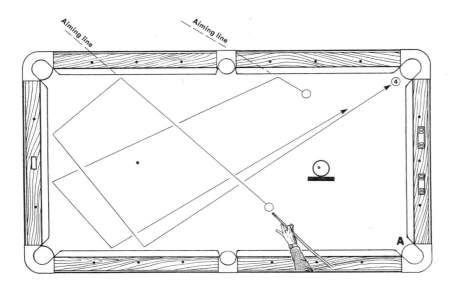

249 Around the table—II

In the previous diagram, the cueball was at corner pocket *A* and was banked three rails to the upper-right corner pocket. Here we have the 4-ball in the jaws. Other balls (omitted) block a direct shot, forcing you to bank. Because you have already determined the distant point, *P*, for a three-cushion shot into the corner, you are home free. From either cueball position, simply aim at the distant point with running English and moderate speed.

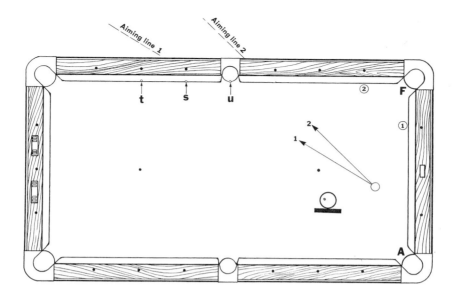

250 Around the table—III

In real life, the target will probably not be the upper-right pocket, *F*, and the cue-ball will not be originating from the ideal position, pocket *A*. In the diagram the problem is to bank three cushions and hit the 1-ball, one diamond down the rail from *F*. (Blocker balls omitted.) First stand behind pocket *A*. Directing a cueball from *A* through *s* to the distant point will send the cueball around the table and into pocket *F*. Since the 1-ball is one diamond down the rail, imagine a line from *A* to point *t*, which is one diamond to the left of *s*. Extend that line beyond the edge of the table and fix in your mind a point about ten or eleven feet away. Go back to the cueball and shoot it at the newly established distant point—aiming line 1—and you will hit the 1-ball off the third rail.

From the same cueball position, can you find the aiming line to hit the 2-ball, which is one diamond away from *F* on the side rail? Stand behind *A* and sight through *s*. Note point *u*, one diamond to the right of *s*. Imagine a line from *A* through *u* and find a distant point eleven feet beyond the table. Shoot the cueball at that distant point along aiming line 2 with running English.

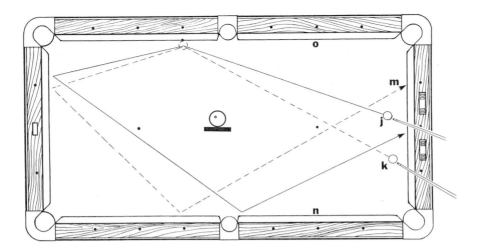

251 Opposite three—I

The opposite-three system enables you to bank a cueball around the table with running English and hit any point on the fourth rail. By "opposite three," I mean the point on the nose of the cushion opposite the third diamond as indicated by the dashed ball in the diagram. The system requires the cueball to contact that point, which can be done from any position by aiming at the center of the imaginary dashed ball. With running English, the cueball will return to the fourth rail at a point symmetrically opposite the starting point. Experience will teach you how much English to use at various banking angles.

Start from *k* along the dashed line and the cueball will return to *m*, which is the same distance from the upper corner as *k* is from the lower corner. Start from *j*, which is two diamonds away from the lower corner, and the ball returns to the same point, two diamonds from the upper corner. Start from *n* on the lower long rail and the cueball will travel to *o* on the upper long rail. It's a useful symmetry.

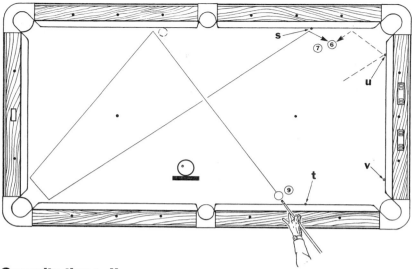

252 Opposite three–II

Here's a position from a game of nine-ball. You have decided that the best way to hit the 6-ball is with a four-rail bank. You decide further that point *s* on the fourth rail is the correct target. The first step is to find the symmetrically opposite point, which in this case is *t*. Stand behind *t* and imagine a line from *t* through the point opposite diamond three (the dashed ball) and note a point about eleven feet beyond the table. Move back to the cueball and shoot it at the distant point with running English.

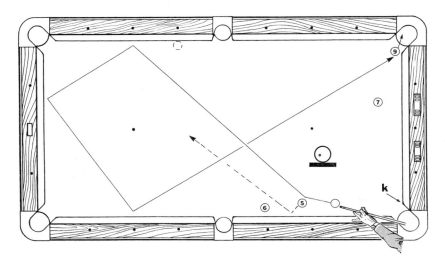

253 Opposite three—III

The opposite-three system can also be used off a ball. Let's say you want to carom off the 5-ball to make the 9-ball with a three-cushion bank. It helps to know exactly where to hit the first rail, and the opposite-three system will tell you. Note that the 9-ball is near the end rail pocket point. Locate *k* near the equivalent point on the lower corner pocket. Stand behind *k,* sight through the dashed ball, and fix a distant point in your mind. Now imagine a line off the side of the 5-ball to the distant point: that's the line the cueball must take to make the shot.

For more, see *Byrne's Wonderful World of Pool and Billiards* (1996), pages 109–113.

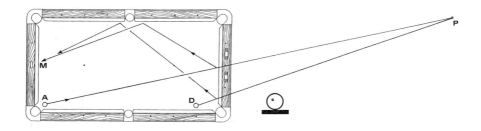

254 End rail first—I

A good end-rail-first system was taught to me by veteran billiard player Don Brink. It is based on the idea that a cueball shot into the end rail with running English (more English, usually, than required for the opposite-three system) will return to a symmetrical point on the other end rail.

In the diagram, a cueball starting from *A* that hits the center of the right-hand end rail will return to the center of the other rail at *M*. Once the distant point, *P,* is established, then to hit *M* from cueball position *D* is simply a matter of aiming at the distant point. Shots of this type are not easy with judgment alone.

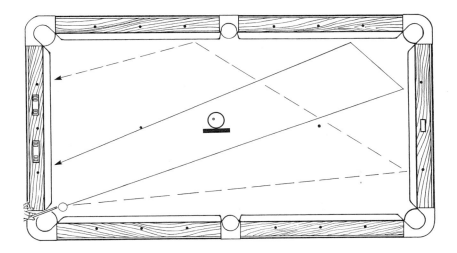

255 End rail first—II

Two more examples will make the concept clear. From the lower-left corner, shooting toward the first diamond down the end rail from the upper-right corner will bring the cueball back to the first diamond up the end rail from the lower-left corner. The dashed line shows that the first diamond up the endrail from the lower-right corner connects with the first diamond down the end rail from the upper-left corner.

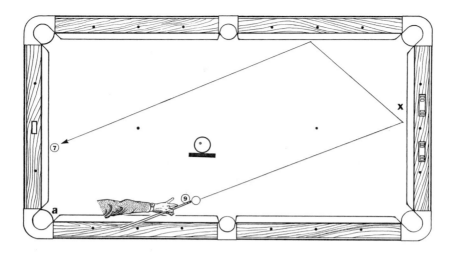

256 End rail first—III

Here is the system applied. How would you hit the 7-ball from this difficult cue-ball position? A three-cushion bank is tough because you would have to bridge over the 9-ball. To use the end-rail system, first imagine that the cueball is in the ideal starting position *a*. Note the location of the 7-ball and find *x*, the symmetrically opposite point on the right end rail. Imagine a line from *a* through *x* to a distant point. Now you can hit the 7-ball off two rails from a wide range of cueball positions by aiming at the distant point.

SELECTED SECRETS 20

A highlight of the annual International Trade Expo sponsored by the Billiard
Congress of America is the Hall of Fame Banquet.

From the Byrne Collection

Here we will take a look at a few strategies useful in eight-ball, nine-ball, and straight pool as well as several little-known special shots.

For more on strategy, see the chapters entitled "How to Run the Table," "The Keys to Winning Eight-Ball," and "The Keys to Winning Nine-Ball" in *Byrne's New Standard Book of Pool and Billiards.*

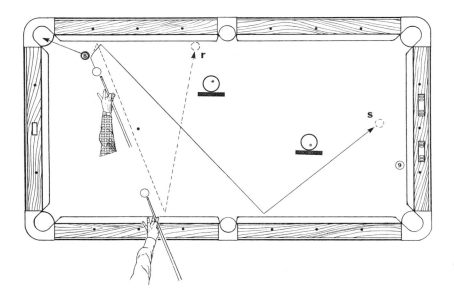

257 English and distance

Whether or not to use sidespin when playing position often depends on the distance between the cueball and the object ball. Sidespin will not make the cueball curve if the cue is perfectly level, but on most shots, given a normal stance and stroke—especially when the butt of the cue must clear the rail—the cue is not quite level, which means that the cueball will curve slightly due to the massé effect.

In the diagram, two cueball positions are shown, one close to the 8-ball, one four feet away. The goal is to cut the 8-ball into the corner pocket and get position on the 9-ball at the opposite end of the table. When the cueball is close to the 8-ball, low right English can be applied with precision and the cueball will be sent on a zigzag pattern (solid line) to *s*. Because the cueball only has to travel a few inches before hitting the object ball, curve is insignificant and the backspin will not wear off (note the slight curve in the cueball's path from the 8-ball to the rail, making it easy to avoid scratching in the side).

When the cueball is four feet away, it's not so easy. From that distance, much more speed is needed to keep the backspin from wearing off, and an allowance in aim must be made to compensate for the curving path. It's better to use no backspin and just slight right English to send the cueball to a point near *r,* (dashed line), from where the 9-ball can be cut in.

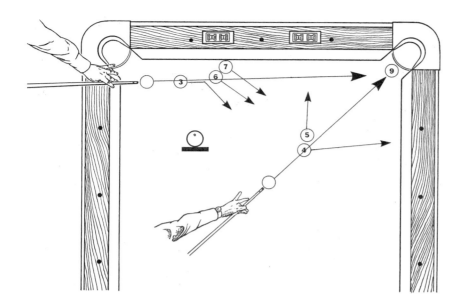

258 Two clearance shots

At the right, the 9-ball is in the jaws. The 4-ball can't be driven into the 9-ball because the 5-ball is in the way. A solution that is often overlooked in games is the clearance shot. Hit the 4-ball squarely with a high ball and watch the cueball follow forward to make the 9-ball. A risk to guard against is using too much speed and following the 9-ball into the pocket for a scratch. Use just enough speed to make the 9.

At the left is a slightly more complicated arrangement. All you have to worry about is hitting the 3-ball in such a way that the cueball will follow and make the 9-ball; the other balls will get out of the way.

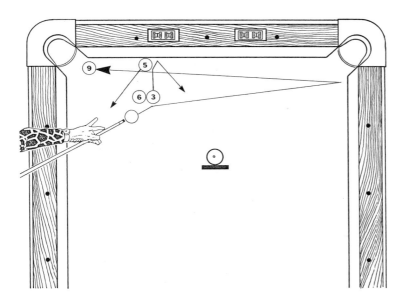

259 A clearance bank

If the 5-ball weren't on the table, most players could make the carom bank off the 3-ball into the 9-ball with good consistency. It's not a very hard shot, even with a blocking 5-ball because the blocker will be cleared away by the 3-ball. The 6-ball is there to prevent a draw directly from the 3-ball to the 9-ball. Chances to make a bank clearance of this type rarely come up, which is not to say they never do. The given position can be used as a challenge. See if a friend can find a way to hit the 3 and make the 9.

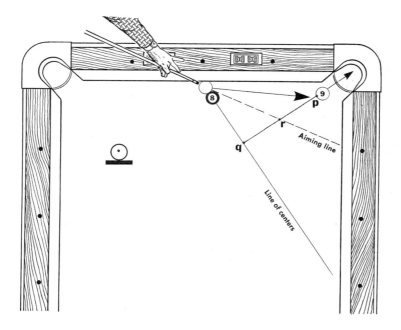

260 Interference system

The cueball is frozen to the 8-ball. The best method of finding an aiming line that will send the cueball through the 8-ball to make the 9-ball was devised years ago by Bob Jewett. First imagine the line of centers, then a line *pq* from the target that is perpendicular to the line of centers. Point *r* bisects *pq*. Aim the cueball at point *r* and you win the game.

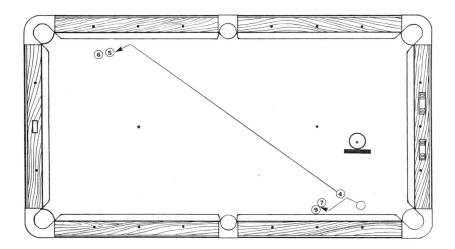

261 Aggressive defense–I

Passive defense is avoiding defeat. Aggressive defense is improving your chances of winning. In the diagram, you have ball in hand in a game of nine-ball. It's easy to find a way to play safe and leave your opponent without a direct shot at the 4-ball, but even if he misses the kick and gives you ball in hand again, a runout is tough because of the two clusters. The winning strategy is to play safe and break up both clusters as shown. Now if your opponent misses the kick, the coast is clear for a runout.

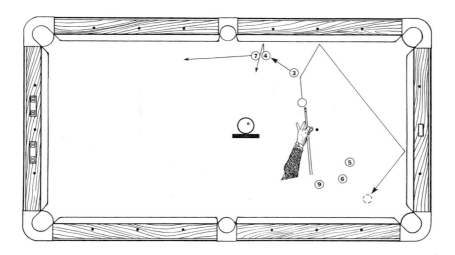

262 Aggressive defense—II

At the right, there is no good way to run out. The 3-ball can be banked in the side, but the 4-ball is locked up by the 7-ball. Of the several safeties that are available, the best one is to drive the 3-ball into the 4-ball, thus eliminating the cluster and at the same time sending the cueball off three rails as shown. Now the odds of winning are greatly in your favor.

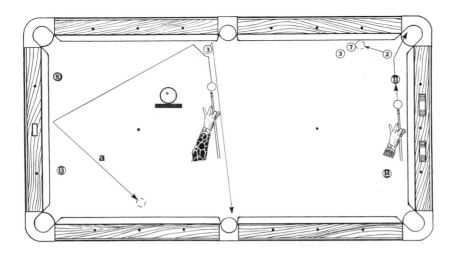

263 Defensive offense—I

Safe leaves are built into some shots. You can shoot with confidence because if you miss you will leave nothing. Other times, you must take action to protect yourself.

At the left is a position from a game of eight-ball. You have the solids and you have decided to bank your last ball, the 3-ball, in the side. Shoot softly and you give the game to your opponent if you miss. The key to the position is to use enough speed to get the cueball past point *a* so that your opponent won't have a decent shot on the 13-ball in case the 3-ball doesn't drop.

At the right, you have the stripes. It's easy to make the 11-ball and get position on the 14-ball with a little backspin. Let's say that there are many other balls on the table (omitted for clarity) and that a runout on your part is not a certainty. To protect yourself from a miss down the line, you can make the 11-ball off the 2-ball, thereby creating a problem cluster for your opponent.

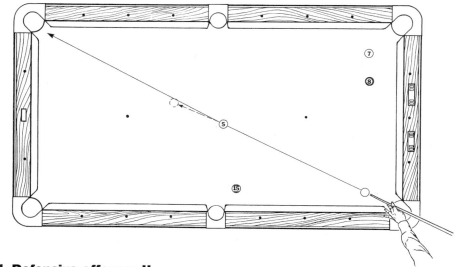

264 Defensive offense–II

The game is eight-ball. The long straight-in shot on the 5-ball is no cinch, but if you make it you have only the easy 7-ball and 8-ball left for victory. A stop shot is a blunder in this position, because a miss enables your opponent to make the 15-ball in the side. Better is to shoot softly and let the cueball drift forward as shown. If you miss, the 5-ball will stay near the corner pocket and your opponent is in trouble.

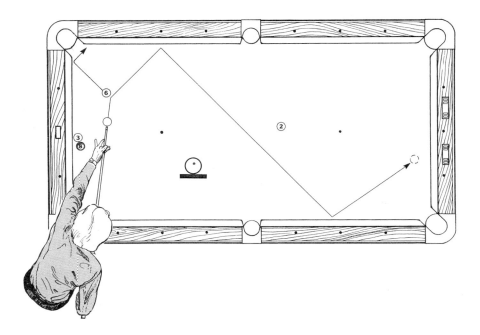

265 Winning options

Here is another eight-ball example. You have the solids and one of your three remaining balls is tied up against the 8-ball. There are many ways to make yourself an overwhelming favorite to win even though your opponent has only the 8-ball left. For instance, you could hit the 3-ball very softly to bump the 8-ball away and force your opponent to bank for the 8, but delicacy is required to avoid selling out. Or you could simply cut the 6-ball into the corner, call safe so you don't have to shoot again, and leave the cueball at the right end of the table. An even better idea is to hit the 6-ball a little too thin, as shown in the diagram, leaving it near the corner pocket. Your opponent would have to be a miracle worker to hit the 8 and leave you without a shot on either the 3- or the 6-ball.

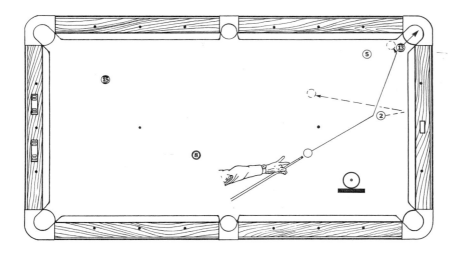

266 A sneaky ploy

Every once in a while in eight-ball it is tempting to hit one of your opponent's balls first. Perhaps you want to create a problem cluster of her balls or to pocket one that is near a pocket so she can't use it for position. Doing either one is a foul, of course, and under most rules gives her ball in hand anywhere on the table.

Pocketing an opponent's ball after hitting one of your own, however, is not a foul. It can be a devastating move. Look at the position in the diagram. You have the solids; she has the stripes. Making the 13-ball off the 2-ball leaves her hooked behind the 5-ball. Without divine intervention, she will lose and the game will be yours.

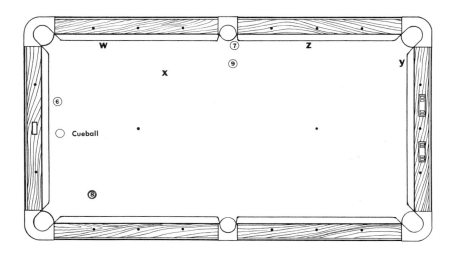

267 Safe or sorry

Should you play safe or go for a winner? The answer depends on your shot-making ability, the quality of the safety you might be able to lay down, and your personality. Some people enjoy taking chances; some think first about protecting themselves.

What would you do in the diagrammed position from a game of nine-ball? There's no way to make the 6-ball and get good position on the 7. One option is to play safe by going off the right edge of the 6-ball to *w* and *x*. If you can hit the 6 really thin, you can send the cueball all the way to the right end of the table without moving the 6 more than a few inches. You'd get a round of applause if you could hook your opponent by zigzagging the cueball to point *y* while leaving the 6-ball at *w*.

The aggressive choice is to shoot a stop shot on the 6-ball followed by banking the cueball two rails, hitting points *y* and *z* and cutting the 7-ball in the side.

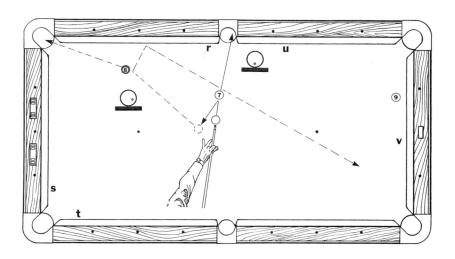

268 **Choice of position**

What's the best way to run out from this position in a game of 9-ball? One approach is a stop shot on the 7-ball followed by a long straight draw off the 8-ball. Some players prefer drawing back a foot or so as shown to leave an angle on the 8. From the position of the dashed cueball, it's easier to get to the right end of the table with low right English using sidespin off the side rail to send the cueball down the table. It's easier because the friction of the cloth doesn't erode sidespin as quickly as it does backspin. Avoid long draws if you can.

Another method is to use follow and leave the cueball at point *r*. From there, cut the 8-ball in and send the cueball to *s, t, u,* and *v*.

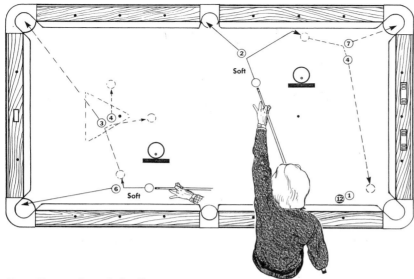

269 Creating a break ball

When there is no break ball, it is sometimes possible to create one by bumping a ball into a favorable position. At the left is a position from a game of straight pool. The dashed triangle shows where the balls will be racked when only one is left on the table. By shooting a soft draw on the 6-ball, the cueball is left in a position to cut the 3-ball into the corner and bump the 4-ball out of the rack to be used as a break ball. (Other balls are omitted.)

At the right, the game is eight-ball or straight pool with extraneous balls omitted. The problem facing the shooter is to break up the 1-12 cluster. One way is to pocket the 2-ball in the side and leave the cueball as shown by the dashed ball. Now the 7-ball can be made and the 4-ball knocked toward the opposite corner pocket where it can be used as a break ball.

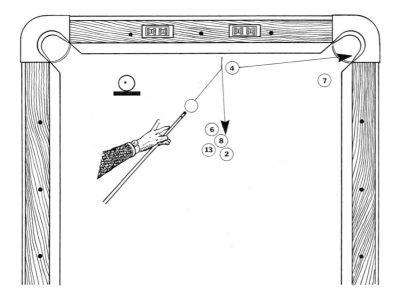

270 Insurance—I

Small clusters of balls can be separated lightly. In a game of straight pool, the four-ball cluster can be broken either off the 4-ball or the 7-ball. The 4-ball is by far the best choice because no matter what sort of leave results, the 7-ball will be available for the next shot.

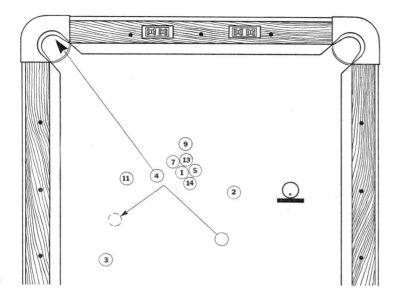

271 Insurance—II

Here is another straight pool position. The six-ball cluster can be broken immediately off the 2-ball, but it's hard to predict what the next shot will be. A wiser choice is to shoot the 4-ball first, drawing the cueball to create an angle on the 11-ball. Breaking the cluster off the 11-ball is safe because the 3-ball can be shot next if nothing better presents itself.

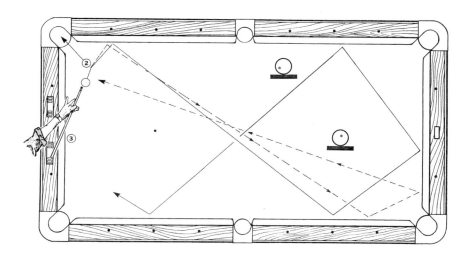

272 **Run around or back around**

The goal is to cut the 2-ball in the corner and get position on the 3-ball. It might be possible in the position shown to hit the 2-ball so softly that it just barely falls into the corner pocket, leaving a severe cut on the 3-ball, but there are two other possibilities.

With extreme left English, the cueball can be made to follow the solid line around the table. The English is reverse off the first rail, then running off the next three. It's a common technique in three-cushion billiards.

The backup pattern, as shown by the dashed lines, is probably more common in pool. The English is running off the first rail and reverse off the next two.

Hard strokes are required for both shots unless the cloth is new and fast.

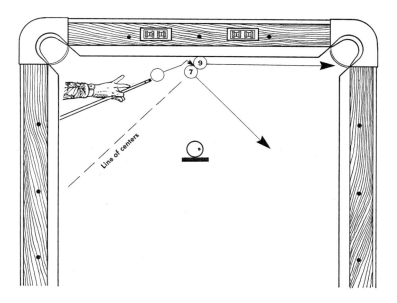

273 Time shot—I

This is so fast it's hard to see what happens. The 7-ball is hit first and the 9-ball goes in. How? It's a time shot, meaning that the second object ball, the 9-ball in this case, is deliberately set in motion. Hit the 7-ball very thin with extreme right-hand spin. The 9-ball begins to leave the rail, but before it moves more than a fraction of an inch, the cueball catches up and knocks it along the rail into the pocket. It looks like magic when it works, which isn't often. I offer it as a novelty, not as a practical shot.

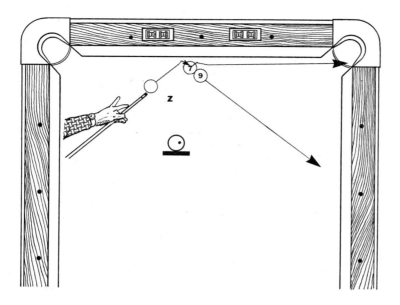

274 Time shot—II

There are two possibilities here. The 9-ball is exactly one ball width from the rail. Position the 7-ball so the 7–9 line of centers passes through the second diamond on the side rail. To make the 7-ball, hit it thin with right-hand English. After the 9-ball is out of the way, the cueball catches up to the 7-ball and sends it into the corner pocket. Again, this is more of a challenge or exhibition shot rather than something worth trying in a game.

A practical shot is available if the cueball is at point z. Hit the 7-ball full and try to make it rebound from the rail and carom off the 9-ball into the pocket. A few tries will teach you the correct speed.

APPENDIX
The Culture of the Game

After immersion in hundreds of pages of technical minutiae, it's easy to forget that billiards and pool have long played a significant role in civilization. Most people not involved in the game, and many of those who are, don't realize how old the game is, what an important part it has played through the centuries in the life of every social class, including royalty, and how often it has appeared as a subject for writers, artists, and composers.

Set aside for a moment the problems of knocking balls into pockets and caroming them off one another, and take a longer, wider view of the game's place in society. In this survey of the game in literature, art, and music, the term *billiards* refers to all cue games, both the pocket and pocketless varieties.

Billiards in Literature

The game of billiards is roughly five hundred years old. Not until the early 1800s, however, did billiards begin to be mentioned in serious fiction, even though by then in both England and France it was hugely popular among the powdered and perfumed members of the royal courts as well as among the odoriferous lower classes. As early as 1591, the English poet Edmund Spenser was denouncing billiards as a "thriftles" game, fit only for London's ruffians and wastrels. The smoothness of a billiard ball was mentioned by Ben Jonson in 1616 in his play *The Devil Is an Ass.* Shakespeare in *Antony and Cleopatra* (1607) cast the Egyptian queen as a billiard player (act 2, scene 5), but he was only kidding; billiard table games can't be traced back beyond the middle 1400s.

The early popularity of the game has always mystified me, given the poor quality of the equipment. Cushions were made of cloth tubes tightly packed with rags, and balls were pushed around with a clubheaded "mace" similar to a shuffleboard stick. How much fun could it have been without cues (not in widespread use until 1800), without tips and chalk (which came in around 1815), without slate beds (about 1830), without rubber cushions (about 1845), and without electric lights (about 1890)? Had I been a ruffian or a wastrel in those days, I would have concentrated on cards, dice, and chess, which aren't so dependent on the equipment.

Rules for billiard games were first given in 1668 in a book titled *La Maison des Jeux Académiques.* The first book in English containing the rules—and other games—was *The Compleat Gamester,* by Charles Cotton (London, 1674). The first book devoted entirely to billiards was published anonymously in 1801 in Bath, England, by "an amateur" and was burdened by this catchy title: *The Game of Billiards—A Philosophical Essay on the Game of Billiards Wherein the Theory Is Minutely Examined upon Physical Principles and Familiarly Exhibited by Easy Transitions from Causes to Effects with Plates Illustrating the Several Propositions Advanced and Practice Shewn in All Its Variety.* Players who wanted solid instruction instead of philosophy had to wait until 1807 for E. White's *A Practical Treatise on the Game of Billiards.*

Casual references to the game can be found in the writings of the great English Romantic poets Byron, Shelley (his second wife, Mary, wrote *Frankenstein*), and Keats. Keats once remarked to a friend that he could imagine a billiard ball taking delight in its own roundness, smoothness, and speed. In 1818, Shelley amused Byron's infant daughter by sitting on the floor with her and rolling billiard balls back and forth. He described the moment in his poem *Julian and Maddalo:*

> *For after her first shyness was worn out*
> *We sate there rolling billiard balls about.*

Byron himself, lame both physically and morally, began one of his many liaisons—with Lady Frances Webster—by playing billiards with her.

References to the game can also be found in early diaries and journals. James Boswell, author of the enduring biography of Samuel Johnson, noted in 1763 that he considered billiards to be "a pretty game" that he rarely played himself for fear of becoming addicted. My favorite diary entry was written by a Colonial legislator named William Byrd II of Westover, Virginia, and is dated

July 30, 1710. Byrd mentioned having made love to his wife and added, "It is to be observed that the flourish was performed on the billiard table."*

Keep in mind that the game before about 1870 was usually played on a large six-pocket table, commonly measuring six by twelve feet, with three or four balls and was a form of what today we call English billiards. Points were scored by caroming the cueball from one ball to another, off one ball into a pocket, or by pocketing a ball. In France, though, pockets had been abandoned to facilitate games based on caroms only.

It's hard to find a stately English manor house today without a stately English billiard room, so it's not surprising that the game appears at least in passing in the works of many stately English (and Russian) novelists, including Jane Austen, Alexander Pushkin, Charles Dickens, William Makepeace Thackeray, Fyodor Dostoyevsky, and Joseph Conrad.

While these famous novelists mentioned the game in their works, none made it the central focus nor were players major characters. That was left to the short-story writers, starting in 1855 with Leo Tolstoy's "Recollections of a Billiard Scorer." I gathered thirty-one relevant short stories in my 1995 anthology *Byrne's Book of Great Pool Stories.* Among the writers who used billiards, pool, or snooker as a theme were H. H. Munro, also known as Saki ("Fate," 1904); A. A. Milne ("A Billiard Lesson," 1911); Stephen Leacock ("Forty Years of Billiards," 1929); John O'Hara ("Sportsmanship," 1934); Wallace Stegner ("The Blue-Winged Teal," 1950); and Walter Tevis ("The Big Hustle," 1955). After the book had gone to press, I discovered "The Greatest Thing in the World," an excellent tale of poolhall lowlifes that Norman Mailer wrote in 1941 when he was eighteen years old.

Walter Tevis's *The Hustler* (1959) was the first mainstream novel about a pool player, and his *The Color of Money* (1984) was the second. The first biography of a real player is my own *McGoorty* (Lyle Stuart, 1972; reissued by Total Sports, 2000). There is also the minutely detailed *Buddy Hall: Rags to Rifleman, Then What?* (1995) by W. W. Woody, which is distinguished from all other books on the game by fifty pages of annotated references to the Bible. A breezy review of the history of billiards together with many interviews with hustlers and tournament players

---

*I am indebted to *William Hendricks' History of Billiards* (Roxana, Ill.: W. Hendricks, 1974) for the early citations.

can be found in John Grissim's 1979 book *Billiards: Hustlers & Heroes, Legends & Lies, and the Search for Higher Truth on the Green Felt.* For a glimpse of the contemporary road player's life, see *Playing Off the Rail* (1996), by David McCumber, who took a tour around the country with pro player Tony Annigoni looking for action... and occasionally finding it. A slightly sanitized look at the life of the great Willie Mosconi (no sex, swearing, or seediness) is *Willie's Game* (1993), by Willie Mosconi and Stanley Cohen.

The first book on the game in the United States was a manual of instruction, Michael Phelan's *Billiards without a Master,* which appeared in 1850. Following that was Dudley Kavanagh's *The Billiard World* in 1869, which contains rules, sketches of prominent players of the day, and a variety of short essays, one of which argues that billiards requires more mental exertion than chess because it requires making your mind up in a hurry. Between 1881 and 1912, the Brunswick-Balke-Collender Company published a half dozen editions of *Modern Billiards* containing instruction as well as year-by-year statistics on matches and tournaments. A very popular instruction book was *Daly's Billiard Book,* by Maurice Daly, which appeared in nine editions between 1913 and 1929, and is still the best guide ever written on how to play straight billiards and balkline.

By about 1920, the two most popular games in the United States for tournament play were straight pool and three-cushion billiards, yet it wasn't until 1941 that a book appeared with three-cushion instruction (Willie Hoppe's *Billiards As It Should Be Played*) and not until 1948 for pool (*Willie Mosconi on Pocket Billiards*). A kind of dam broke in the last quarter of the twentieth century: from 1975 to 2000 more American books of instruction were published than in the whole previous history of the game in this country. The Library of Congress catalog lists nearly 250 books under the "billiards" heading. Log on to *Amazon.com* and browse "billiards" and you'll find around 180 titles; but more than half are out-of-print and available only on the secondhand or rare-book markets.

Collecting books on billiards has become a popular pastime, and scarce volumes, such as the 1827 Paris edition of François Mingaud's *The Noble Game of Billiards,* fetch $1,500 and up. Several collectors have amassed astonishing libraries. Roger Lee in England has 150 books on snooker and English billiards alone. In Vienna, Heinrich Weingartner—player, table maker, room owner, and billiard museum curator—has over 800 books in his collection. At the Billiard Archive in Pittsburgh, curator Mike Shamos is the proud owner of over 1,000 volumes and is doggedly pursuing the hopeless goal of finding a copy of every book on the game ever published in any language. The overwhelming majority of the books, of course, are devoted to rules of the various games and instructions on how to play them.

But manuals of instruction are seldom Literature. Many of the early how-to-play books, in fact, were written in a style that if not literary was at least purple, and when not purple, preachy. Consider this example from *The Game of Billiards,* by Michael Phelan (1857), one of many that could be quoted:

> The game is peculiarly in harmony with the mechanical genius of our people; it combines science with gymnastics, teaching the eye to judge distances, the mind to calculate forces, and the arm to execute with rapidity and skill whatever the mind and eye combine to dictate for its execution; it expands the chest while giving grace and elegance to the form, and affords even to the illiterate mind a practical basis for the appreciation of mathematical and geometric truth.

The greatness of Mark Twain, an avid fan of both pocket and carom billiards, can be seen in the fact that he was one of the few nineteenth-century writers who escaped from the stuffy and convoluted style that covered almost everyone else like syrup. In 1867 he made a trip to Europe and sent letters back to several American newspapers that were published in book form two years later as *Innocents Abroad.*

From Paris, Twain wrote:

> At eleven o'clock we alighted upon a sign which manifestly referred to billiards. Joy! We had played billiards in the Azores with balls that were not round, and on an ancient table that was very little smoother than a brick pavement—one of those wretched old things with dead cushions, and with patches in the faded cloth and invisible obstructions that made the balls describe the most astonishing and unsuspected angles and perform feats in the way of unlooked-for and almost impossible "scratches," that were perfectly bewildering. We had played at Gibralter with balls the size of a walnut, on a table like a public square—and in both instances we achieved far more aggravation than amusement. We expected to fare better here, but we were mistaken. The cushions were a good deal higher than the balls, and as the balls had a fashion of always stopping under the cushions, we accomplished very little in the way of caroms. The cushions were

hard and unelastic, and the cues were so crooked that in making a shot you had to allow for the curve or you would infallibly put the "English" on the wrong side of the ball. Dan was to mark while the doctor and I played. At the end of an hour neither of us had made a count, and so Dan was tired of keeping tally with nothing to tally, and we were heated and angry and disgusted. We paid the heavy bill—about six cents—and said we would call around some time when we had a week to spend, and finish the game.

In his later years, Twain played many hours a day. His daughter Suzy wrote, "Papa's favorite game is billiards, and when he is tired and wishes to rest himself he stays up all night and plays billiards; it seems to rest his head." Before Twain died in 1910, he said, "The billiard table is better than the doctors."

Florid writing and sermonettes disappeared from billiard books after the turn of the century. In addition, the game itself nearly disappeared from novels; serious writers were preoccupied with two world wars and the depression. After World War II, the game became grist for writers again. The two pool novels by Walter Tevis, *The Hustler* and *The Color of Money,* became popular movies starring Paul Newman. Pool scenes can be found in *Cry Tough,* by Irving Shulman (1949); *Billiards at Half-Past Nine,* by Heinrich Böll (1961); *Hard Rain Falling,* by Don Carpenter (1966); *Boys and Girls Together,* by William Goldman (1964); and *Billy Phelan's Greatest Game,* by William Kennedy (1978).

Leave us not forget *The Wedding Gamble* (1996), by western romance writer Cait Logan. Her yarn is set in the 1880s and features the ravishingly beautiful pool hustler Cairo Brown, "the billiard-playing queen who had beaten Montana's best" and who ends up in a showdown match with herself as the prize.

Lovers of the game who have any interest in its colorful history should not be without three recent books that often rise to the level of Literature. One is the extraordinary *Hustlers, Beats, and Others* by the late Ned Polsky, a sociologist's look at the poolhall subculture and the profession of hustling; there's a glittering nugget on almost every page. The book was published in 1967 by Aldine Publishing Company; an expanded and updated edition was released by the Lyons Press in 1998. Another is *The Illustrated Encyclopedia of Billiards* by Mike Shamos. It's a 300-plus page alphabetized reference work that makes accessible a tremendous amount of previously buried information about every facet of the game. Included is an eight-page color insert that provides a glimpse of the rich tradition of billiards graphics. The first edition, from Lyons & Burford, Publishers, is dated 1993; an expanded and revised version was published in 1999 by the Lyons Press.

The third "must have" book is one of the most stunning volumes ever published on any game or sport: the *Billiard Encyclopedia* by Victor Stein and Paul Rubino. It's pricey, but this beautiful, large-format celebration of the game is worth the investment. Replete with color illustrations, half of the pages are devoted to history, and half to cues, which are treated as an art form. If you want a massive billiard volume published to the highest art-book standards, this is for you. The contents are presented in narrative rather than alphabetical form, so be sure to get the 1996 (or later) edition, which has an index. You won't find this in bookstores. For information, write to Victor Stein, 3801 Hudson Manor Terrace, Riverdale, NY 10463, or visit *www.billiardencyclopedia.com.*

One of America's finest contemporary novelists is Richard Russo, who broke into the first rank of writers with *Mohawk* in 1986, and has gone on to write such works as *The Risk Pool, Straight Man* (academia was never funnier), *Nobody's Fool,* and *Empire Falls.* There are several pages in *The Risk Pool,* his second novel, describing pool-playing among high school boys, beginning with this provocative paragraph (with which I will end my survey of billiards in literature):

> I have heard expressed more than once a theory that claims a direct relationship between skill at pocket billiards and a corresponding lack of skill in matters sexual. I lean toward the theory, especially if you happen to be talking about adolescents. In Mohawk, all the best pool shooters had reputations as ladies' men, but I could never see where these reputations were earned or deserved. There was the general sense that guys who hung around the pool hall were men of the world, and stories of conquest travel even better over green felt than calm water. But I never knew back then, nor do I know now, a real stud with a pool cue who could carry on a normal conversation with a woman.

Billiards in Art

In a small café in Arles, France, in 1888, there was a billiard table destined to live forever. The café is gone now and so is the table, but paintings of it by Vincent van Gogh and Paul Gauguin are among the most famous in the world. Van

"The Night Café" (1888) by Vincent Van Gogh
© Francis G. Mayer/CORBIS

Gogh reported in a letter to his brother, Theo, that he had stayed up three nights working by gaslight on the painting, now called *The Night Café*. The table and a man in white take center stage; a few idlers are secondary. Gauguin put a local woman with an enigmatic smile in the foreground of his painting; behind her is the table, and behind the table is—but I can use the words of the artists . . .

"I have tried to express," Vincent wrote to Theo, "the terrible passions of humanity by means of the red and green. The room is blood red and dark yellow with a green billiard table in the middle; there are four citron-yellow lamps with a glow of orange and green. Everywhere there is a clash and contrast of the most disparate reds and greens in the figures of the little sleeping hooligans in the empty, dreary room, in violet and blue. . . . The white coat of the landlord, awake in a corner of that furnace, turns citron yellow, or pale luminous green."

A few months later he wrote: "Gauguin is working on a canvas of the same night café I painted, but with figures seen in the brothels. It promises to turn out beautifully."

"In the Café in Arles"
(1888) by Paul Gauguin
© Alexander Burkatowski/
CORBIS

Gauguin also wrote letters from Arles. "I have also done a painting of a café which Vincent likes a lot and myself less. Actually, it's not my subject and the vulgar local colors don't suit me. . . . At the back red wallpaper and three prostitutes, one bristling with paper hair-curlers, the second seen from behind wearing a green shawl. The third in a scarlet shawl; on the left a man asleep. A billiard table—in the foreground a rather carefully executed figure . . . Across the picture runs a streak of blue smoke."

Gauguin's painting, titled "In the cafe at Arles," is in the State Pushkin Museum of Fine Arts in Moscow. To see the Van Gogh, you need only go to New Haven, Connecticut, to the Yale University Art Gallery. If you want to buy the painting, take at least forty million dollars.

Other famous painters have made use of billiard tables. Edgar Degas turned away from ballet dancers long enough to paint *The Billiard Room at Ménil-Hubert* in 1892. Man Ray did several versions of *La Fortune*—a surrealist billiard table combined with a desert landscape and cumulous clouds—in the late 1930s; one can be found at the Whitney Museum in New York City. Do you like the jagged angles and hard-to-fathom compositions of the cubist school? Then Georges Braque is the man for you; he did four billiard paintings in the late 1940s.

Not so famous is Jacob Lawrence, a black American painter whose *Pool Parlor* (1942) is a striking composition of players, tables, balls, and hanging lights;

it's at the Metropolitan Museum of Art in New York City. Other Lawrence billiard paintings hang in the Boston Museum of Fine Arts and the Hirshhorn Museum in Washington, D.C.

For color reproductions of the above paintings and for more on the artists, see the five-page article "Artistic Billiards," by Mike Shamos in *Billiards Digest* magazine, December 1992. The article also shows a 1750 engraving by Probst, an 1822 aquatint by Cruickshank, and an 1865 lithograph by Daumier. Also see "The Art of the Archive" by Shamos in the March 2003 edition of *Billiards Digest*. In *The New Illustrated Encyclopedia of Billiards* (2002) by the same author is an eight-page insert with color illustrations by Thomas Rowlandson (1823), Jean Droit (1910), C. H. Mecham (1857), and unnamed artists dating back to 1710. The largest collection of billiard artwork and original paintings in the United States is held by the Billiard Archive, in Pittsburgh, Pennsylvania—Mike Shamos, curator.

A veritable banquet of billiard art is served up in *The Billiard Encyclopedia: An Illustrated History of the Sport* (2nd ed., Blue Book Publications, 1996) by Victor Stein and Paul Rubino. This 550-plus page tome contains over 800 illustrations, 520 in full color, chosen from 30,000 photographic images in the collection of the authors. From the British Museum comes a very early painting: three Dutch aristocrats playing a billiard table game, by Adriaen van de Venne (1589–1662). Another splendid plate is *Interior d'Une Grande Salle* by Bartholomeus van Bassen (1590–1652). A half page is devoted to a wonderful oil by Louis-Léopold Boilly (1761–1845), owned by the Hermitage Museum in St. Petersburg, Russia: men, women, children, and dogs are gathered around a billiard table in a splendid scene that has been much imitated. The faces of the onlookers and the silken gowns of the women are beautifully rendered and the scene is full of life. For the front endleaf of the book, the authors chose a great painting of a public billiard room by Jean-Siméon Chardin (1699–1779) from The Musée de la Ville de Paris.

A number of paintings have become popular as wall hangings in billiard halls or home game rooms. From 1880 to 1910, *Vanity Fair* commissioned artists to create a series of colored lithographs that were offered to subscribers as supplements to the magazine. Three showed dignified gentlemen holding cues and standing rather stiffly by billiard tables. Two were politicians and one was British billiard champion John Roberts, Jr. Two are by an artist known as Spy, the other is by one who signed himself "T." Prints struck from the original plates change hands for between $150 and $200.

Also popular as wall art are reproductions (not original prints) of three paintings by Archie Gunn, who was commissioned by Brunswick-Balke-Collender Company in 1910 as part of an advertising campaign for new table models. In each painting, a table is being used by a woman in elaborate, flowing gowns. The titles are "A Graceful Stroke," "Avoiding a Kiss," and "Beauty of Billiards."

A memorable example of advertising art is a poster copyrighted in 1901 by Koehler & Hinrichs of St. Paul, Minnesota, purveyors of bar furniture, billiard tables, bowling alleys, glassware, wholesale delicacies, and butchers' supplies. Believe it or not, the unknown artist worked all of the above into a wild scene of a black bull charging into a room that has a bar, three billiard tables, a bowling alley, and display cases. A surprised billiard player is trying to defend himself with his cue while the bull is being restrained by a man who, judging from his tool belt, is a butcher.

When you step down from fine art to graphic art, the universe of billiard images is staggeringly huge. For hundreds of years billiards has been a theme for advertisers, political cartoonists, caricaturists, manufacturers of billiard products, and tournament program and poster artists. Line drawings from newspapers and magazines before half-tone cuts took over are a rich source of billiard artwork. In the nineteenth century, billiard matches and tournaments were treated as important news and were often illustrated by drawings both large and small. Books on the game are another place to find fine billiard art, especially old books. An example is *Billiards* (London and Bombay: Longmans, Green and Co., 1896), by Major W. Broadfoot, which is illustrated by drawings of uncanny photographic realism by Lucien Davies. Several Davies renderings are used as chapter headings in *Byrne's New Standard Book of Pool and Billiards.*

Billiard art isn't limited to products associated with the game. In the last ten or fifteen years, billiard motifs have appeared on a wide variety of merchandise, from undershorts to men's ties, from wristwatches to cummerbunds, and billiard settings are used in both print advertisements and television commercials to push everything from beer to insurance.

Postcards are a surprisingly large field for collectors of billiardiana. Reproductions of the Arles café paintings by Van Gogh and Gauguin and works by other famous artists are often available on cards sold in museum gift shops or through mail-order billiard supply houses. Rare original cards from a hundred years ago range in price from five to fifty dollars. There are probably between 4,000 and 5,000 collectable postcards worldwide. Most show billiard rooms, tables, or other billiard products; many are humorous cartoons (a popular theme is a bungling player ripping the cloth or spilling drinks with one end of his cue or the other), and some are purely artistic.

There is a tremendous amount of European graphic art relating to billiards that has never been seen in the United States and only recently has come to the attention of American collectors. Much of it is in the Vienna museum maintained by Heinrich Weingartner, who has been a serious collector for forty years. The covers of the magazine he has edited since 1988—*Billard: mit dem offiziellen Teil des Billardsportverbandes Österreich*—are often devoted to displaying gems from his incredible collection of images: fine art, engravings from obscure publications, comic cartoons, renderings of royal billiard rooms, paintings of the game being played by circus clowns, pigs, monkeys, and even insects, and scenes of coffeehouses and cafés with billiard tables. Examples can be seen in *Byrne's New Standard Book of Pool and Billiards* and in the present work.

Graphic designers and fine artists are sometimes commissioned to create covers for books about billiards. See for example the painting by Joel Iskowitz for the dust jacket of the 1979 hardcover *The Howard Hughes Affair;* by Max Ginsburg for the cover of the 1984 paperback edition of *The Hustler;* by Jim Dietz for the cover of the 1984 paperback edition of *The Color of Money;* by Doug Henry for the 1987 dust jacket of *The Body in the Billiard Room;* by John Ramhorst for the cover of the 1992 paperback *Lush for Life;* by Richard Tuschman for the dust jacket of the 1996 hardcover *Playing off the Rail;* the second cover painting by Elaine Duillo for the 1996 paperback *The Wedding Gamble;* the front cover for the 1975 paperback *Rumble Fish* (artist not named); and the Wendell Minor paintings for my four how-to-play books (1978, 1982, 1990, and 1996).

Magazines occasionally hire artists to illustrate articles on billiards. See, for example, the four paintings by Dickran Palulian that appear with my article in *Sports Illustrated,* Oct. 9, 1978. The same magazine ran an article on March 20, 1961, by Jack Olsen on pool hustling that featured three wonderful drawings by the late, great Saul Steinberg of *New Yorker* fame.

A contemporary artist whose billiard paintings are available in limited-edition prints, note cards, and as originals is Dutchman Nico Vrielink, who lives in France and is represented in this country by New Deco of Boca Raton, Florida. French painter Guy Buffet has done several amusing café scenes with well-stuffed, bow-tied businessmen gathered around a billiard table with their cigars and cues. American artists who have done billiard-related paintings include Aldo Luongo, Michael Young, Philip C. Curtis (his *The Game* hangs in the Phoenix Art

Museum), and Marcia Yerman (for a 1988 women's tournament poster sponsored by Blatt Billiards of New York City). The late Wayne Thiebaud did several striking canvases of spheres that remind me of pool balls, though that's probably not what he intended.

My favorite contemporary billiard paintings are by Brad Holland of New York, one of the most influential graphic artists of the last fifty years. He did them for the March 1988 edition of *Frankfurter Allgemeine Magazin.* Six were reproduced in glorious color in the December 2001 edition of *Billiards Digest* magazine.

A few of the artworks mentioned in this survey can be seen on the Web at *billiardencyclopedia.com; newdeco.com; byrne.org;* and *3cushion.com.* For a look at what's available in the field of pop poster art for billiard room walls and home game rooms, check out *absolutesportsworld.com; billiard fanatic.com; billiardart-gallery.com;* and *billiardlibrary.com.*

Billiards in Music

Name the famous Broadway musical comedy that mentions both three-cushion billiards and balkline. Hint: It also mentions Dubuque, Iowa, my hometown. If you answered *Pajama Game,* you are wrong, even though that musical is set in an Iowa pajama factory once owned by author Richard Bissell's family. Correct is Meredith Willson's *The Music Man.*

One of the most enduring of American musicals, *The Music Man* opened in 1957, ran for 173 weeks, and is periodically revived. Its two best-known songs are "Seventy-Six Trombones" and "Ya Got Trouble." *Trouble,* you will remember, starts with *T,* which rhymes with *P.* What starts with *P? Pool!*

Lovable con man Harold Hill steps off the train in River City, Iowa, looking for a way to convince the locals that they should buy his line of band instruments, uniforms, and lessons. He finds it when he discovers that a pool table has replaced the town's only billiard table. As people gather around him one by one, he states his case to Ewart Dunlop, the grocer.

Hill warns Dunlop that a disaster threatens the community by the presence of a pool table, and launches into his famous song about trouble in River City.

The surprising feature of Hill's spiel is the claim that billiards is okay; *pool* is the problem. Gentlemen play billiards, he claims, bums play pool. He is proud to be a billiard player, mighty proud, and considers golden the hours he spent with a cue in his hand. To make a tough shot in three-cushion takes "horse sense and a cool head and a keen eye." Scoring in balkline takes "judgment, brains, and maturity." Not so in pool, the professor explains to the townfolk. "Any boob," he says, "can take and shove a ball in a pocket / and I call that sloth!"

The professor points out that the road to degradation starts with medicinal wine from a teaspoon, moves on to beer from a bottle, and ends with kids playing pool for money. Those kids, he predicts darkly, will turn into cigarette fiends and one night will leave the pool hall for the dance hall, where "shameless men and scarlet women and ragtime" will turn them into jungle animals.

One wonders how much this popular musical comedy has contributed to the notion expressed by so many city councils that a pool hall really *will* be a problem.

Another well-known billiard musical reference occurs in *The Mikado,* one of Gilbert and Sullivan's fourteen light operas. The piece is set in 1750 and was first produced in 1885 at the Savoy Theatre in London. Like *The Music Man,* it is almost always being performed somewhere in the world. The farcical plot is carried along by characters with such names as Nanki-Poo, Pooh-Bah, and Yum Yum. The all-powerful Mikado, Emperor of Japan, is a man who enjoys making sport of convicted criminals by subjecting them to deliciously appropriate punishments. As he puts it:

It is my very humane endeavor
To make, to some extent,
Each evil liver
A running river
Of harmless merriment.

My object all sublime
I shall achieve in time—
To let the punishment fit the crime—
The punishment fit the crime.

He then describes the sentences he metes out to various kinds of miscreants, like those who write their names with their fingers on train windows. Pool hustlers (sharps) are in special jeopardy. (In the following lyric, "finger-stalls" are splint bandages for injured fingers; "spot barred" is a restrictive rule in English billiards.)

The billiard sharp who anyone catches
His doom's extremely hard—

He's made to dwell
In a dungeon cell
On a spot that's always barred.
And there he plays extravagant matches
In fitless finger-stalls
On a cloth untrue
With a twisted cue
And elliptical billiard balls.

The last third of the 1800s seems to have been an especially fertile period for billiards in popular music. Five thematic songs were published that I know of: "I Don't Play at Billiards Now," "I Won Her Heart at Billiards," "Billiards and Pool," "It's Billiards on the Brain," and the almost identically titled "Billiards on the Brain." The last-named was published in 1869 by Kunkel Brothers of St. Louis; on the cover of the sheet music is a painting with eleven people around a billiard table and two dogs playing underneath (dogs were once an oddly common feature in billiard art). The painting can be seen in *Byrne's New Standard Book of Pool and Billiards* (1998), page xxvi.

"It's Billiards on the Brain" was published by Wm. A. Pond & Co. of New York. The composer of the simple melody hid behind the *nom de plume* "A. Carom," but the author of the amusing lyrics bravely revealed herself to be Grace Carleton. She wrote one version for gentlemen and one for ladies.

Gentlemen's Version

1. *Of all the pleasant games we play,*
        What game can equal this?
   We practice it by night and day
        Its joys we never miss.
   Where e'er we go, it is our lot
        To hear this one refrain:
   "Come in and play,"—the world has got
        This billiards on the brain!

   CHORUS
   The balls go rolling round the table
        In this little game;
   It matters not which ball you hit;

The count is all the same.
We take our cues and chalk them up,
And carom on the red;
But very oft we make a scratch
And hit the white instead.

2. *The game of life resembles it—*
   We often make a "miss,"
At other times we make a "hit,"—
   And frequently we "kiss."
Some new beginner plays near by
   He lifts his cue again,
And gently pokes you in the eye—
   That's billiards on the brain! [CHORUS]

3. *Quite oft while looking at a friend,*
   Who makes a splendid "run,"
The game is drawing to an end,—
   You think it splendid fun,
When suddenly, before you know,
   You feel a twinge of pain,—
A ball comes bouncing on your toe—
   That's billiards on the brain! [CHORUS]

4. *Young Jones he was as nice a man,*
   As ever you did see,
And when the game he once began,
   He counted splendidly.
He played all night, he played all day,
   With all his might and main;
Alas! He died!—the people say,
   Of billiards on the brain! [CHORUS]

Ladies' Version

1. *Of all the horrid games I know,*
   That one is hateful quite,
To which the men in crowds will go,
   And play at, day and night.

> I wonder what the charm can be,
>> It must be great, that's plain,
> For young and old, it seems to me,
>> Have billiards on the brain. [CHORUS]

2. I had a beau, so nice and sweet,
>> He used to call each eve,
> And every time our eyes would meet
>> His smiles I would receive.
> But now he talks of "shots" so fine,
>> As if he were insane;
> I really think he does incline
>> Towards billiards on the brain! [CHORUS]

3. There's Mister Jones, who lives next door,
>> He comes home very late,
> And vows he couldn't come before,
>> All owing to his state.
> His wife believes "He's at the store,"—
>> Alas! the case is plain,—
> It's only just one noodle more
>> With billiards on the brain! [CHORUS]

4. Take my advice, young maiden, pray,
>> When beaus have distant grown,
> And smell of "smoke" by night and day,
>> And leave you sad and lone;
> Just say, "To wed is not your plan,"
>> Nor bid them call again;
> A girl's a fool to wed a man
>> With billiards on the brain! [CHORUS]

Other songs in the 1800s made passing reference to the game, usually in a cautionary manner, as in "Don't You Go, Tommy," published by H. De Marsan of New York, words and music by C. T. Lockwood. One verse will suffice:

> Now listen, my boy, now mind what I say
> Don't spend all your money and time in that way,
> There's no one but idlers that lounge about so,

I beg of you, Tommy, don't go.
We're feeble and old, your mother and me;
And kind as a mother has been should you be.
To whiskey shops, billiards, and cards bid adieu,
I beg of you, Tommy, don't go.

Thanks to Roger Lee, a collector and dealer in billiardiana (a word he coined) who sent me a photocopy of the sheet music from England, I can quote the first verse and chorus from "I Don't Play at Billiards Now," written in 1895 by Harry Boden, music by W. H. Noel: (Note: John Roberts Jr. was England's great champion at the time; A "marker" is a person who keeps score for the players.)

It's long ago since I first thought I'd learn to play at billiards;
I bought a cue and case and paid a lot of ready tin;
The billiard markers said he'd make of me a second Roberts
And teach me theoretically the way to always win.
I trusted him implicitly (although he was a boozer)
He took his oath I'd make a player in a year or two.
I'd thirteen lessons every week at half a crown an hour
But the only thing I've learned is simply how to chalk a cue.

CHORUS
I've lost all my ambition—the fascination's gone
I feel repugnant to the game somehow;
It's no use to idly chatter
I've been HAD, that's what's the matter
So I don't play at billiards now.

Many musicians have enjoyed playing pool and billiards—pianist Leonid Hambro and violinist Pinchas Zuckerman come to mind. Most notable of all, of course, is Wolfgang Amadeus Mozart (1756–1791). In 1985, American Gramaphone released a compact disc entitled *The Mozart Collection* containing highlights of nine Mozart orchestral pieces as played by the City of London Sinfonia, John Rutter, conductor. The artwork for the CD jewel-box consists of a billiard-cloth-green background on which are superimposed three staffs of music and three billiard balls. The author of the liner notes had this to say:

With enthusiasm and delight, Mozart played billiards, the kinetic movement of the red and white balls proving an outlet for his intense creative energy. Mozart played the game at home with other musicians, composers, pupils, and friends. And he played alone. At his own billiard table, as at the piano, the delicate hands of Mozart moved with grace and ease, for it was acknowledged that when Wolfgang played billiards, he usually won.

His extreme concentration and retentive memory allowed him to compose whole works in his head...during walks, at meals, and at billiards. Cue in hand, leaning toward the flat, green field, the mind of Mozart could move his musical notes about like billiard balls.

There's a lovely scene in the 1984 Milos Forman film, *Amadeus*. While a Mozart score plays in the background, the composer (played by Tom Hulce) is bent over his billiard table writing music with one hand and idly rolling a ball back and forth with the other. There's a knock on the door, and when he looks up the music stops, and the viewers realize that what they were hearing was flowing from the composer's pen.

Mozart died at the age of thirty-six. An inventory of his second-floor apartment in Vienna at that time listed a billiard table, five balls, and twelve cues. The windowless room housing the table was lit by one lantern and four candles.

Pool is referred to in many twentieth-century pop songs. George Fels of *Billiards Digest* magazine remembers "Small fry, struttin' by the pool room" (when they should be in a school room), from a 1938 musical called *Sing You Sinners,* music by Hoagy Carmichael, lyrics by Johnny Mercer. In 1983, Huey Lewis and the News released their best-selling album *Sports.* On the album cover, a pool table is front and center, and the six members of the group are pictured inside The 2 A.M. Club in Mill Valley, California, a fixture in the Marin County Tavern Pool League. I know because I was living in Mill Valley at the time.

Fels gave me the names of these tunes that at least mention the game: "Late in the Evening," by Paul Simon; "Maggie May," by Rod Stewart; "Main Street," by Bob Seger; "Juanita," by Bruce Springsteen; "Chuck E.'s in Love," by Rickie Lee Jones; and "(Looking for) The Heart of Saturday Night," by Tom Waits. More than passing mention can be found in "Rack 'em Up," by Johnny Lang, and "Don't Mess Around with Jim," by Jim Croce, which describes a mark's bloody revenge on a hustler. Willie Mosconi appears for no discernible reason on the George Thorogood video "Bad to the Bone." Perhaps readers can add to the list.

The movements of a cueball were once set to classical music, namely "The Dance of the Hours" from act 3 of Amilcare Ponchielli's opera *La Gioconda*. Between 1991 and 1993, Lucasfilms produced thirty-two episodes of *The Young Indiana Jones Chronicles*. The formula called for old Indiana Jones, played by George Hall, to reminisce about his adventures as a youth, played by Corey Carrier (ages 8–12) and Sean Patrick Flanery (ages 17–21). A dozen of the episodes are now on videotape and being sold as two-hour movies; they are shown occasionally on the Family Channel or USA. I was hired to shoot trick shots at a tavern in Novato, California, for a segment titled "Florence—May 1908." The show begins with Old Indy climbing off a bar stool to show some young whippersnappers how the game of pool should be played. In a sharply edited sequence, the cueball dances around the table in perfect *con brio* synchronization with Ponchielli's sprightly music. Only my hands are seen. As this is written in 2003, "Florence—May 1908" is not yet one of the programs available for purchase. For information on the series, log onto *www.google.com* and search for "Young Indiana Jones."

INDEX

Perfect your game with these books on pool and billiards by Robert Byrne, member of the Billiard Congress of America Hall of Fame

Byrne's New Standard Book of Pool and Billiards
Updated and expanded with new material on strategy in eight- and nine-ball, trick shots, and billiard memorabilia, this comprehensive guide to cue games remains "the definitive work on pool and billiards" (*National Billiard News*).
ISBN : 0-15-600554-9
Price: $20.00

Byrne's Advanced Technique in Pool and Billiards
This invaluable companion volume to *Byrne's New Standard Book of Pool and Billiards* contains clear explanations and helpful diagrams for experienced players ready to lift their game to a higher level.
ISBN : 0-15-614971-0
Price: $21.00

Byrne's Treasury of Trick Shots in Pool and Billiards
This book contains more than three hundred ingenious exhibition shots—some easy, some not—all fully described. "The most complete book on the subject I have ever come across." (Jimmy Caras, four-time World Champion).
ISBN : 0-15-614973-7
Price: $20.00

Byrne's Wonderful World of Pool and Billiards
An insider's absorbing look at the world of pool and billiards, its champions and hustlers, with tips on how to hone your skills and become a winner.
ISBN : 0-15-600222-1
Price: $18.00

Byrne's Book of Great Pool Stories
Robert Byrne introduces thirty short stories covering 150 years of cue games, from Pushkin and Tolstoy to Milne, Stegner, and Tevis.
ISBN: 0-15-600223-X
Price: $18.00